POLITICAL TURMOILS OF SAMBALPUR (ODISHA)ZAMINDARIS DURING 1857 MUTINY

Dr. Dadhibaban Mishra

AUTHOR'S NOTE

The present work is a recast version of a Project financed by University Grants Commission, New Delhi to which the author owes a deep dept of gratitude. It proved to be an uphill, but nonetheless interesting and provoking, task in so far as many hitherto unknown sources came to limelight to revisit earlier works and make the present one. The participation of the people in general and the *Zamindars,* the *Maufidars, Garhtteas* and *Gauntias* of the feudal order in particular of a comparatively hinterland of the country - the Sambalpur Tract (Odisha) during the 1857 Mutiny and aftermath is a landmark. It may be corroborated from the statement of Maj. A.B. Cumberlege, Deputy Commissioner, Sambalpur (1864-66):

> I do not wish for a moment to be considered an alarmist but the circumstances of the little district of Sambalpore isolated as it is and surrounded on every side by the territories of the feudatory Chiefs and Zamindars, render it possible for events to happen there, which could not occur in any other part of India. It behoves us therefore to ensure more than an usual amount of caution and to guard against every contingency.

The problems in the path of investigation were many and significant and, honestly speaking, a few of them could not be solved even at the present state of information. Be that as it may, considerable labour has been done to gather pieces of information by extensive travels in the nook and cranny of the Zamindaris and interacting with people, to analyze them in proper perspective and fill up the hiatuses in the developments of eventful five years (1857-62) as far as possible.

(i)   The major and most important part of source materials constituted archival materials – British Government letters, records, reports and other documents preserved in various archives and offices. All the works, which are -of course- a few , produced so far in either English or Oriya are based on them. That is to say, the few published books/articles go by the evidences of the writings of the British people. Thus far we have been seeing things as those official sources have shown us. That is, we have been seeing things in British eyes. And thus far, the books produced have remained lopsided. No attempt has been made to verify the facts that have come down to us till date on the basis of non-official British and/or indigenous sources. The works are more or less in the nature of documentation with brief descriptions by writers and often without interpretations. It has rightly been observed:

To a casual reader these Dispatches and reports covey an impression, that those opposing the foreign rule were all backward and anti-socials. These Dispatches and notes do not hesitate to brand the leaders of the movement and their followers as "Dacoits". All civilian gatherings to demonstrate opposition to foreign occupation as "Militancy" 'insurrection' and the participants as "insurgents". But after a thorough and critical scrutiny of these "letters and Dispatches" one can come across the reality on the ground. In case, certain information faithfully recorded and conveyed to the higher formation finds place, the person or persons responsible were reprimanded. These Dispatches would be returned for fear of getting permanence in the Records of the office. The Imperialists knew the art of drafting letters that could safeguard the interest of their imperial master. One has to bear in mind that foreign power, or a vested interest to preserve its privilege and promote its popularity, will spare no pains to carry public opinion in its favour.

The imperialists then as now therefore, must develop an acute knowledge of the art of dissemination of information. This art is all the more necessary when there are several contenders on the ground. The British representing their interest through the East India Company were therefore to count critics at home, in Europe and America, as well as the existing powerful political forces in India. They had to learn and teach their agents the art of drafting notes and dispatches lest they might have to face criticism from their own authorities. This aspect need be borne in mind when one attempts to study these documents. The historians or their scribes hold the view that the British Empire was "the result more of a chance than a design"?

It is very disheartening to realize that not a single diary by a native can be counted or made available to the researcher. Unfortunately, there was no other systematic organization, engaged in documenting the events, other than that of the Imperialists. Hence one has to study these records and documents very thoroughly and interpret, taking the prevalent geo-political situation and the social system of the time.
(Mishra, R.K.: *Surendra Sai*, from Author's Desk, pp. viii-ix)

A very very small amount of representative accounts written by individual officers has been made available. No account of a soldier, a sepoy, a memoir, a non-participant's account and non-official contemporary accounts – as in the case of other regions – has become known relating to the Tract. The journals of the period is nil and, if published in other vernaculars those have not come to our notice.

(iii)   So a comprehensive account is a desideratum and, the present investigation is an attempt to fill in the hiatuses, as far as possible, by searching new materials and interpret them in the perspective of the spirit of the age, aspirations of the people and, the contrary aspect of intention of the British Government.

Despite the large number of works produced on the Mutiny relating to its occurrence and progress in different parts of the country by now, the role of the people and the *Zamindars* of Sambalpur who have played a significant role and kept the flame of the Rebellion burning for more than five years has been sidelined, may be, due to non-availability of records to the authors or disregard to the history of a hinterland by scholars.

Even those latest works like N.K. Sahu's *Veer Surendra Sai* (Bhubaneswar, 1985) and R.K. Mishra's *Surendra Sai, Pioneer of a Complete Revolution* (Sambalpur, 2002) have followed the pioneer work of A. Dash's *Life of Surendra Sai* written in 1962-63 on the basis of the British records.

(iv)   The living scions of the *Zamindars* have not only not kept any record or document - which was, of course, difficult in those days, when paper and writing instruments were not easily available and most of the people were unlettered - but also they are ignorant of the names – what to speak about the attainments of their forefathers who suffered and sacrificed themselves in the Rebellion in the Tract. A few families, like that of Ghens and Pahadsirgida worship a few traditional weapons once in a year only without knowing who used them when and why while no material is to be found in other *Zamindars'* houses.

(v)   It is lamentable that the Governments of India and Odisha have not known even the names of those *Zamindars,* till very late, when some of their names like that of Hatte Singh - were published in *Who's Who*

(vi)   *of Indian Martyrs*, Vol. III, New Delhi, 1973. Hatte Singh was one of the two men of Odisha who was deported to Kalapani (Andamans) where he died also; but his name was in oblivion till the seventies of the previous century.

(vii)   Many of the memorials like the fortresses or stone works constructed by the rebels on various hills or hill-passes have been destroyed, leaving little traces behind to enable one to form a bare idea of military bases of the rebels fighting in the dense and inaccessible hilly and jungle land – particularly the Manikgarh region, Gurrah Pahad, Tandul Pahad and Baghdhula Pahad in the Sunabeda hill range in the Jonk river valley of present Nawapada district in the later phase of the rebellion or Debrigarh, the centrally located and strategic fort on the Barapahad hill of Lakhanpur *Zamindari* in the early phase.

Such was the fate of the missiles, weapons and guns of the time – many of which have been lost to posterity now, a few have been preserved in some *Zamindars'* houses or Sambalpur University Museum and the like.

(viii)   Many of the areas of operations of the rebels have become impenetrable and/or invulnerable due to depredations of elephants and, of late, Maoists. Some areas have been covered with wild plants, sand

(ix)   and soils and have allowed but a little scope to scholars for maintaining field

books.   Present day inhabitants have a little information of the places and

events that shook their areas..

(x)   Of late, records have been collected and classified at various places like New

Delhi, Kolkata and Bhubaneswar on 1857 Mutiny.   The Indian Council of

Historical Research brought out recently *1857 : A Select Bibliography*

(compiled by P.N. Sahay) which has been of some use to study the turmoils

of the Tract in the context adjacent regions of the contemporary period. 'The

complete version' that has been planned on the line of 'regional classification

which will itemize titles with an all-India coverage, followed by four regional

Sections on Northern, Eastern and Central India and on other parts of India'

(ibid, Introduction, Sabyasachi Bhattacharya) will go a long way to further

unfold new vistas of research.

(xi)   All that seem to have been lost is not lost. There came a silver lining in the

darkness of cloud. Since last three decades, there has been sporadic effort

for search of new facts at different levels – Government, Institutional and

Personal and, quite a good corpus of new facts preserved or known by people

came to light which shed welcome light on many an obscure aspect

(xii)   In 2009, the birth bi-centenary of the principal leader of the Rebellion (1857-1862) Surendra Sai has been observed at different fora. A few Souvenirs, Journals and Write-ups were brought out on the occasion. The activities of other leaders, role of associates of Surendra and some other people were discussed at length – though often without references. Scholars evinced sincere interest and worked on the one or the other aspect of the Rebellion of 1857. as Some amount of information relating to activities of the people as well as *Zamindars* of the *Zamindaris* became available. A group of scholars dedicated themselves to the collection folk-songs (given in Appendix-I) which replenish facts gleaned from more dependable sources, besides enlightening us of new facts whereas some other groups moved across the Tract to organize meetings, see places and gather more facts. The present author seized the opportunity of the celebrations at different places and moved through the nook and cranny of the Tract in the itinerary of fact-finding missions in which to some extent he was benefited.

The book has been presented in 8 Chapters. Chapter 1 : **Zamindaris of Sambalpur Tract – Physical Features and Historical Antecedents Bearing on 1857 Mutiny** – delineates on the peculiarities of the geographical features of the *Zamindaris* of the Sambalpur Tract. The hill systems and the forests and the riparian system have been outlined to provide a reader an idea about their bearing on, or the background of, the disturbances for about five years (1857-62), which are comparatively unknown to people both of the Tract and outside. The significant roles of hill-passes and hill-military bases of the rebels, which have contributed significantly to the continuance of the Rebellion have been assessed and their importance discussed in the Chapter.

The historical antecedents of *Zamindaris* of Sambalpur kingdom from its foundation in last quarter of 16th century to annexation in British Empire in 1849 has been traced. The circumstances leading to the creation of *Zamindaris* at different times have been delineated. Sidelight has been shed on the development of Land Tenure System which was the pivotal factor creating circumstances that led to the Rebellion.

Chapter 2 : The narrative **The Zamindaris : A Prelude to 1857 Mutiny** is about the political developments of Sambalpur kingdom during the four decades (1817-57) preceding the Mutiny. The claim for the throne by a few claimants of which Surendra Sai was one, following death of Maharaja Sai, the king of Sambalpur and its disregard by the British authorities on two occasions when they made Mohan Kumari, the deceased's queen and Narayan Singh rulers in 1827 and 1833 respectively – made the claimants resentful and they organized the tribal people and *Zamindars* in rebellion.

The 30's and 40's of 19th century witnessed a number of disturbances in which *Zamindars* of Bheden, Jharsuguda, Pahadsirgida, etc. played vital role. The topsy-torvy land tenure system, which changed traditional rent-free grants into revenue-paying and deprived the grantees of their rights and privileges – in the aftermath of British occupation – paved the ground for future disturbances. Thus when the Tract was in a state of readiness for turmoil, the Mutiny broke out and became a conflagration into which the Tract made a deep dive

Chapter 3 : **The Early Phase of the Rebellion** started at Sambalpur in September/October 1857 with the arrival of Surendra Sai after he was set free from Hazaribag jail by the mutinous soldiers. During its occupation of the eight years (1849-57) the British Rule had become thoroughly unpopular and discredited and the people and *Zamindars* jumped into the fray of the rebellion. The non-violent nature of the Rebellion, the exhibition of patriotic zeal by all sections of people, the resentment of the Brahmins and village-worshippers and *Zamindars, Garhtteas* and *Gaunteas* following revocation of, or taxation on, rent-free land, and importantly, the demand for restoration of Sambalpur kingdom under Surendra Sai by all and sundry – the majority of tribal people, the Brahmans, the *Zamindars* and, significantly, by the kings of surrounding kingdoms like Khariar, Bamra, Bindra-Nawagarh, Sarangarh etc. and, last but not the least, the emergence of *Zamindars* as leaders were the hallmarks of the Rebellion. The disturbed state of law and order made the Government desperate. The period was marked by disturbances, encounters between rebels and army and, successes of the rebels except in the Battle of Kudapali (December 1857).

Chapter 4 : The **Fully Fledged Rebellion.** The three years (1858-60) was the period of extensive military preparations and operations on the part of the British Government on the one hand and tough resistance and fighting of the rebels on the other, was the most important feature of the period. The landmarks of the period were attack on Kolabira and capture and execution of its *Zamindar* (February, 1858), severe fighting at Singhora pass between Cap. Shakespeare and rebels under members of Ghens *Zamindar* family, British attacks on Debrigarh and Pahadsirgida and death of Cap. Woodbridge in the hands of Pahadsirgida *Zamindar.*

Stern measures adopted by Commissioner Cockburn of Cuttack like execution of some *Zamindars*, confiscation of *Zamindaris*, setting up of military outposts on the border as well as interior areas, warning against help to rebels and imposing fines on Ruling Chiefs – like that of Patna etc. and, importantly, the reign of terror unleashed by the Deputy Commissioner, Sambalpur W.R. Forster made it difficult for the rebels to operate efficiently.

The rebels shifted their bases of operation to rebel-friendly peripheral regions like Nawapara-Khariar, Bindra-Nawagarh and other border areas of Sambalpur and Raipur and, carried on their depredations against British-friendly people and created havoc. The major incidents were the killing of the *Zamindar* of Deori (July 1860), raid on Khullari, rebel operation against the British under patronage of Raja Krishna Chandra Singh Deo of Khariar and Tanwat *Zamindar* Lal Shah at Manikgarh, Tandul, Baijhula and other hilly regions, attacks on Patna, Bamra, Raigarh, Sarangarh,. The policy of 'blood and iron' of Deputy Commissioner Forster was of no avail. He was ultimately discredited and removed in March 1861.

Chapter 5 : **The Turning Point** in the Rebellion of Sambalpur came following the appointment of Maj. H.B. Impey as Deputy Commissioner.. He realised the futility of further military operations against the rebels to restore law and order situation and, decided to adopt a policy of moderation and conciliation towards the rebels. The policy passing through many odds, ups and downs, finally brought successes. His attempt to bring all rebel leaders to surrender to

Government was, in fact, a remarkable feat of achievement. He tried to convince both the people and his higher authorities about the necessity of the policy in which he became successful ultimately. He prevailed upon the Commissioner, Cuttack who, in his turn, made Government of India to release a Proclamation of Amnesty in October 1861. Despite strong reactions to his policy from many of both Government and rebel sides – with the support of Commissioner R.N. Shore – he paved the way for surrender of the rebels. The *Zamindars* of Rampur, Patkulunda, Kolabira, Kharsal, etc. and some other rebels surrendered and, as promised by Impey, their estates were restored to them. Besides on their surrender, some *Gauntias* like Loknath Panda and Mrityunjaya Panigrahi were generously rewarded.

Impey and R.N. Shore made direct communication and negotiations at great personal risk with rebels. The policy resulted in the surrender of principal rebel leaders like Mitrbhanu, Surendra's son (January, 1862), Dhruv and Udant – Surendra's brothers, Hathi Singh – *Zamindar* of Ghens and finally Surendra, Khageswar Dao of Lakhanpur, Khageswar (Nunha Dewan) and two brothers of Janardan Singh, ex-*Zamindar* of Pahadsirgida. Only two of the notable leaders Kunjel Singh of Ghens and Kamal Singh of Lakhanpur remained at large.

Chapter 6 : **The Turn of the Tide** came after the death of Maj. H.B. Impey in December 1863 and the appointment of Maj. A.B. Cumberlege as

Deputy Commissioner, Sambalpur in January 1864. It brought about reversal in the policy of appeasement and conciliation of the former to one of revenge, arrest and punishment of the latter. Another notable feature of the period was the transfer of Sambalpur Tract from the jurisdiction of the Commissioner of Orissa Division to that of Chhatisgarh Division in April 1862, which brought in its trail the reactionary attitude of Central Provinces officials towards Impey's policy. That resulted in hunting down the rebel leaders, like Kamal Singh and Kunjel Singh, who had not surrendered and, arresting those like Surendra and others who had surrendered and settled. Forged documents and evidences were prepared at a rapid pace and, within a few days those were made ready. Finally, all those were arrested and despatched to Raipur for trial. All of them had been punished by the Sessions Court in June 1864. Although they were acquitted and set free by the Judicial Commissioner, they were detained vide Regulation III of 1818 and, thereafter confined in Asirgarh fort jail in East Nimar District of Central Provinces.

Chapter 7 : Succinct Profiles of the **Movers and Shakers** of the Rebellion of the *Zamindaris*, whose references have been made in one context or the other, have been delineated. The roles that they had played at different times and occasions thus would be properly understood.

Chapter 8 : The findings of the investigation have been recorded in this Chapter titled Conclusion.

Two Appendices (i) Glimpses of 1857 Mutiny in the Folk Songs of Sambalpur Tract (ii) Facsimiles of some letters have been provided thereafter.Glossary for non-English or indigenous terms and Bibliography are the last two features of the Contents.

The dissertation is illustrated with 5 nos.of maps.

ACKNOWLEDGEMENT

University Grants Commission, New Delhi, for the kind financial assistance.

National Archives,NewDelhi, Orissa State Archives,Bhubaneshwar, West Bengal Archives, Madhya Pradesh State Archives, Bhopal, Nagpur Secretariat Record Room, Nagpur, Board of Revenue, Cuttack, Revenue Divisional Commissioner's Record Room, Sambalpur for permission to use of records and take Xerox copies.

G.M. College Library, Sambalpur, Government College Library, Bhawanipatna, Orissa State Library, Bhubaneswar, Odisha Sanskritik Samaj Library, Sambalpur, Central Library, Sambalpur University, Burla, Mahant Ghasidas Museum Libray, Raipur, Kanika Library, Ravenshaw University, Cuttack for permission to read books and take photocopies.

Prof. (Dr.) H. Panda, Co-Investigator of the Project, Raja Saheb J.P. Singh Deo of Khariar, Prof. (Dr.) G.P. Guru, Ex-D.P.I. (Schools), Orissa, Dr. D.K. Gaur, Sr. Lecturer in History, Attabira College, Attabira, Sri J.B. Panda, Lecturer in Education, Bheden College, Bheden, Sri B.P. Nanda, Journalist and Social Activist,

Ms. A. Gartia, Lecturer, T.T. College, Ghatagaon, Keonjhar, Dr. S.K. Pradhan, Lecturer, Hills College of Teacher Education, Naharlagun, Arunachal , M.N.C. Pillai, a Retd. steno for rendering different kinds of assistance.

Zamindar Families of Ghens, Borasambar, Lakhanpur, Pahadsirgida, Patkulunda, Kolabira, Bheden, Rampur, Bindra-Nuagarh, Tanwat for allowing visits to their houses and providing some information.

Villagers of Khinda, Rajpur, Bargaon, Talab, Tabla, Rengali (Sambalpur district), Bheden, Pahadsirgida, Kudopali, Lakhanpur, Tope (Bargarh district), Tanwat, Jhalap, Nuapada, Tikrapada, Dungripali, Komna (Nawapara district), Deori, Khullari, Nawapara (Raipur district, Chhatisgarh) for accompanying the Investigator to various sites and providing hospitality.

'Vagisvari'   Dr. Dadhibaban Mishra
Lane R-3, J.M. Colony,
At/P.O. Budharaja,
Sambalpur – 768004 (Odisha)

LIST OF MAPS

(i)   Location of Zamindaris of Sambalpur Tract.

(ii)   Gurhjat Mahals

(iii)   Cuttack Division

(iv)Strategical Sites and Battle Fields in 1857-58

(iv)   Strategy of Surendra Sai

CONTENTS

CHAPTER 1

ZAMINDARIS OF SAMBALPUR TRACT

PHYSICAL FEATURES AND HISTORICAL ANTECEDENTS

BEARING ON 1857 MUTINY

Sambalpur Tract of Odisha, in the context of the present investigation, refers to the kingdom of Sambalpur, ruled by the Chauhana dynasty from about 1570 to 1849 A.D., when it was annexed to the British Empire of India by the Doctrine of Lapse or Escheat. The Tract comprised the present districts of Sambalpur (minus Rairakhol or Redhakhol sub-division which was a Feudatory State and Kuchinda sub-division which was a part of former Bamanda State), Bargarh and Jharsuguda.

The total area of the Tract was 10,213 sq.kms located within $20^0 43'$-22^0 11 North Latitude and $82^0 39'$ – $84^0 15'$ East Longitudes. It was bounded by present Chhatisgarh State on the west, Balangir District (ex-Patana kingdom) and Sonepur District (ex-Sonepur kingdom) on the south, Angul and Deogarh (ex-Bamanda State) Districts on the east and Sundargarh Distinct (ex-Gangpur kingdom) on the north.

There were as many as 16 *Zamindari*s in the Tract on the eve of 1857 Mutiny[1]. Those were, with their extent, Ghens (104 sq.kms), Kharsal (73 sq.kms), Lakhanpur (642.1 sq.kms), Pahadsirgida, Bheden or Beseikela (374 sq.kms), Borasambar or Padampur (2178.19 sq.kms), Bijepur (214.97 sq.kms), Patkulunda (21.54 sq.kms), Mundomahal (18.13 sq.kms) and Barpali (254 sq.kms) – all in present Bargarh district; Kolabira (720 sq.kms), Rampur (386 sq.kms) and Machida (25.9 sq.kms) – in present Jharsuguda district; Loida (64 sq.kms), Kodabaga (75 sq.kms), Rajpur (93.24 sq.kms), of present Sambalpur district[2]. The total area under the *Zamindari*s covered an area of 1,791 sq. miles (4538.69 sq. kms). The biggest of them is Borasambar with an area of 841 sq. mils (2178.19 sq.kms) and the smallest was Patkulunda having an area of 6 sq. miles (21.54 sq. kms). The total number of villages in the *Zamindari*s were 1,042[3]. The total *Zamindari* area was about 118,30,000 acres but the proportion of land which was cultivated was not known[4].

Physical Features

The Tract is described as consisting of 'a wide expanse of fairly open country fringed by forest-clad hills as well as a series of low hill ranges of extremely irregular shape'. Present Sambalpur and Bargarh Districts of the Tract forms an 'undulating upland varying in elevation from 479 feet (146 m) to 750 feet (228.6 m) above sea-level excluding hills and tablelands' and, 'it is much broken up by rugged ranges of hills, and is traversed in all directions by drainage channels mostly leading from the hill ranges to the Mahanadi and its tributaries'. Broadly speaking, the Tract is a hilly country, clad with dense forests and a considerable area consists of 'ground cut up by ravines or broad sandy ridges'.

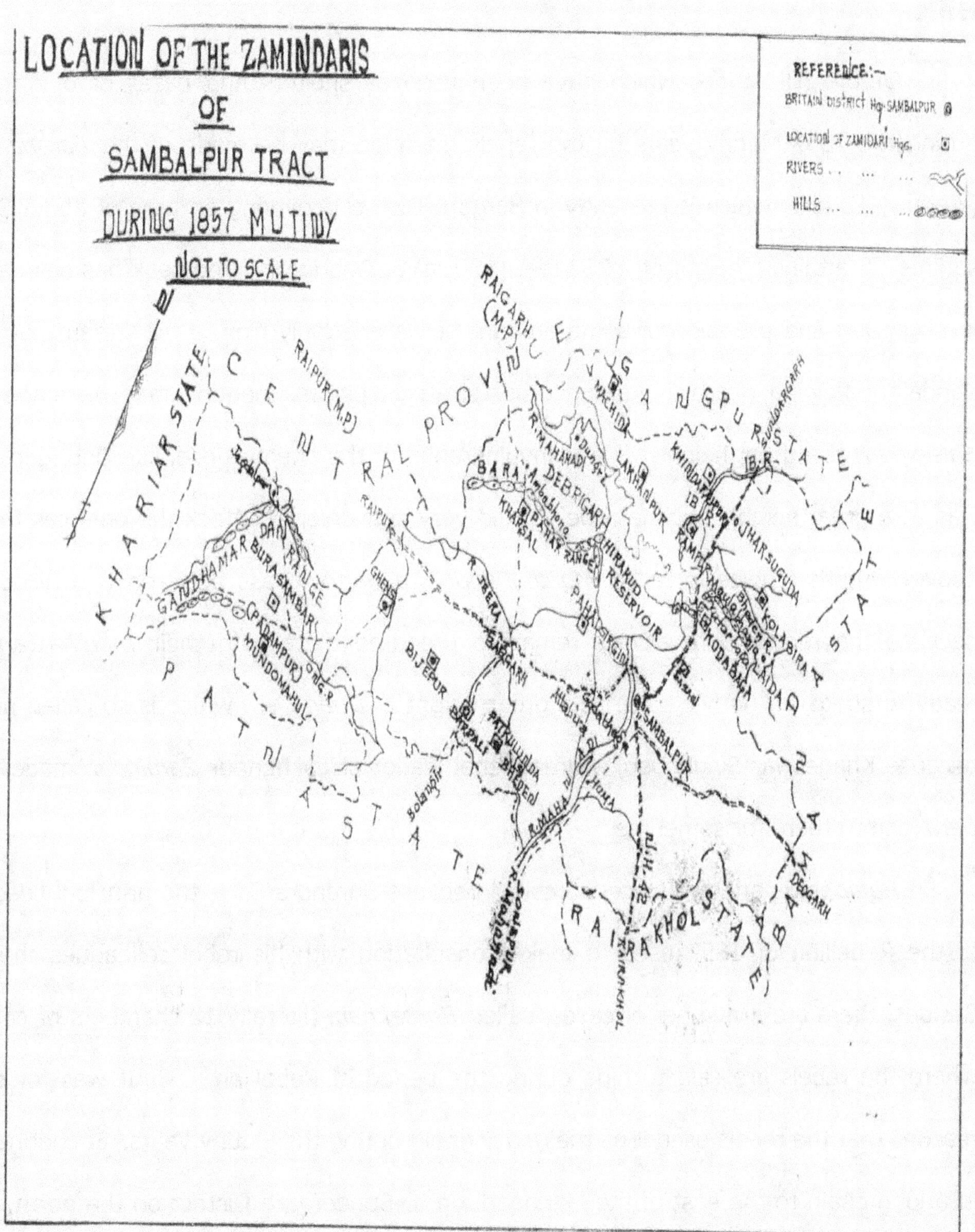

LOCATION OF THE ZAMINDARIS
OF
SAMBALPUR TRACT
DURING 1857 MUTINY
NOT TO SCALE
REFERENCE:-
BRITAIN DISTRICT Hqr SAMBALPUR
LOCATION OF ZAMIDARI Hqs.
RIVERS
HILLS
KHARIAR STATE
CENTRAL PROVINCE
RAIPUR (M.P)
RAIGARH (M.P.)
GANGPUR STATE
SUNDARGARH
GANDHAMARDAN RANGE
BURASAMBAR
BARA DEBRIGARH
MACHIDA
LAKHANPUR
KHINDA
IB R.
BARA PAHAR RANGE
KHARSAL
HIRAKUD RESERVOIR
JHARSUGUDA
KOLABIRA
GHENS
R. MAHANADI
PAHARGARH
AMBABHONA
KHODABANDA
LAIDA
PADAMPUR
MUNDONAHUL
BIJEPUR
R. TEKRA
BARGARH
PATKULUNDA
BARPALI
BARDEOL
SONEPUR
R. MAHANADI
HIRLI
HATIBARI
SAMBALPUR
BOLANGIR
R. ONG R.
N.H. 42
RAIRAKHOL STATE
BAMRA STATE
DEOGARH
R. BHEDEN

Hills

Of the hill ranges which have been used as shelters and bases of operation during the 1857 Mutiny years by the rebels, mention may be made of the *Barapahad* (literally, 12 hills, which is presently in Bargarh District) covering an area of about 800 sq.kms. It attains a height of 2,267 feet (690 m) at Debrigarh. The peak has plain and level ground and provision of some amount of water-supply from a hill stream named Kandajhor flowing nearby. Among other strategic places, mention may be made of *Satanigarh* at a great height. It was invulnerable for the enemy since, like Debrigarh, it was at a great height, but the rebels could very conveniently attack the enemies from above. Another place is called *Morchabandha,* a narrow pass between two hillocks, because the rebels were always remained prepared there with their *morcha* (army ready to strike). Another place at a great height is *Duan Dera* which is so called now because Khageswar Singh Deo, a great rebel leader of Lakhanpur *Zamindari* made his *dera* (camp) there for sometime.

Rajabasa is another place, so called because Surendra Sai – the principal Leader of the Rebellion of 1857 used to make consultation with his rebel colleagues there. Besides, there are a number of caves, called *Barbakhara* (literally 12 chambers or cells) where the rebels are said to hide during the period of Rebellion.   It was for the reasons that the rebels used it as their stronghold during the Mutiny years. It continues in a long chain to the east of the Mahanadi up to Sundergarh District on the north. It provided a number of hideouts for the rebels. It was suitable for guerrilla mode of warfare against the British army which found it difficult to carry on its military operations against the rebels in the hilly and forest-clad terrain.

The second hill-range is the *Gandhamardan* running on the south of present Bargarh District. It separates Bargarh from Balangir District. The rivers Ong and Suktel have come out of it – the former runs through Bargarh, Balangir and Sonepur and, the latter through Balangir and Sonepur. Both meet the Mahanadi near Sonepur.

The *Papanga* hill range in Bargarh district is as wide as it is long. It was under Bheden (Baseikela) *Zamindari*. The hill and the villages in environ have been the theaters of encounters of the British army and the rebels on some occasions.

Of the principal hill ranges of present Sambalpur District which have contributed to the encounters of the rebels of the Mutiny, mention may be made of *Lamb Dungri* or *Jharghti* lying to the north of Sambalpur town. Its highest peak is 516 meters above the plain. There are a number of broken ranges to its south, important of which are the *Munder* which has a height of 476 meters and *Sunari* which has a height of 472 meters. The *Maula-Bhanja* (literally, uncle-nephew) lies to the north-west of Rengali along the Rengali-Katarbaga road. The Budharaja hill in the heart of present Sambalpur is said to have provided shelter to the principal rebels of the Mutiny time. There are two other hills named *Gotwaki* and *Guja* about 16 Kms to the north-west of Sambalpur. The *Lahanda* hill lies to the left of the road from Bargarh to Sambalpur.

The Rairakhol portion of the Tract is 'on the whole hilly and hills form continuous ranges' almost in all cardinal directions and the central part as well. The northern hill range extends between the border of the ex-State Baudh and Kisinda valley, covering about 260 Kms. The Western and eastern ranges are *Paria, Ghumel, Buria pahar, Khajurdiha* etc.; the northern ranges have *Pali, Derajuri, Sursuri, Bhaleshwar* and *Bhalodari,* while the central range extend from Sambalpur to Athmallik of Angul district.

The hilly and rough terrain had no road for travel. The passages between two hills or the lowest point in the ranges of hills provided the tracks for movement for the people. Such passage was known as *ghāṭ* or *ghāṭī.* Among the famous of them were *Jharghati, Singhora ghati, Badpati ghati* located on Sambalpur to Ranchi, Nagpur and Cuttack routes respectively. There were secret passes through which one who knew the routes could escape easily whereas a stranger would be lost in the forests or be a prey to bandits or wild beasts. The fortresses were built on and near the *ghats.* Debrigarh on the Barapahar in Lakhanpur *Zamindari*, another at Jharghati, another at Singhora near Sohela were impenetrable to the offensive party. On the other hand, the people in the area could defend themselves by sliding or putting big boulders, dropped from above the hills, on the passage and, thus creating problems for movement of the enemy. They could eliminate an entire group of enemies by releasing a few boulders from the hilltop. During the Rebellion, in fact, they tied big pieces of stones with 'siall' creepers on the sides of hillocks and cut them to roll down when the British forces were campaigning. It caused great hardship to the enemy. Their file formation, strategy, guns and weapons were of no avail in such circumstances. The guerrilla warfare, which was quite suitable to the terrain, probably counted to some extent for prolongation of the encounters and continuation of the Rebellion in the Tract for a longer period.

Rivers

The rivers, rivulets, streams and nullahs criss-cross the landscape, thus making it impassable during rainy seasons and making it difficult for movement of goods, arms and ammunitions and armed forces. Besides, some areas remained inhospitable, vulnerable to mosquito and insect bites and tropical diseases.

The Mahanadi makes the Tract a central basin. It enters the Tract through its north-west and flows to south-east through Bargarh and Sambalpur districts. The bed of the river in the Tract is full of rocks and rapids. 'In spite of rocks and rapids, boats can ascend the river, and before construction of the Bengal-Nagpur Railway (renamed South-Eastern and, of late, as East Coast Railway) it was the main outlet for the produce of the district to be carried in boats to Cuttack. Its course in the Tract is full of huge masses of boulders and stones and thus made it dangerous for navigation. It is described by Charles Grant[5] as 'the terror of boatmen standing up in midstream and realizing the exact notion of Scylla and Charybdis'.

The principal tributaries of the Mahanadi in the Tract are the Ib flowing through Gangpur State (present Sundargarh District) and Sambalpur, the *Bheden* flowing through Kolabira *Zamindari* and Sambalpur *Khalsa*, the *Jira* which comes from the Barapahad and flowing through Phuljhar (Chhatisgarh) and Bargarh meets the Mahanadi at Turum of Bargarh District, the *Danta* is the main tributary of the *Jira* and, the villages of Bheden and Remenda which have played a part in the Mutiny against the British are on its bank, the *Ranj* river which takes its origin from near Sohela of Bargarh District is another tributary of the Jira. Patkulunda – a village after which a *Zamindari* is named – is on its bank. The *Uttali* flows between Bijepur and Padampur and Bijepur

Zamindari was known as Uttal after the name of the river. The Malti river flowing by some 10 Kms from Sambalpur town contains Kudopali and Manesar on its bank. Among other rivers mention may be made of *Jhain* which originates from the Barapahad and falls in the Mahanadi, the *Ghenshali* – a tributary of the Ong flowing between Sohela and Padampur, the *Kulari* and the Girishal etc.

Rivers, particularly the Mahanadi, have been the lifelines, for travel, trade and commerce, movement of armies when no convenient land connectivity among places had been available from earliest time till the coming of the British. It is said that there was an ancient route from the Yamuna valley in the north to Kalinga in the south – which ran from Kausambi (Allahabad) to Koshala through Bilaspur-Raipur and thereafter along the Ong valley through Borasambar, Bargarh up to Sonepur[6]. P.Acharya[7] has informed us that one may take the route from Sonepur via Sambalpur-Bonai-Keonjhar-Khiching-Dhalbhum to Dandebhukti (Midnapur, West Bengal). The route from Cuttack to Nagpur passed through Sambalpur, which was used by both the Marathas and the British for movement of armies[8]. T. Mottee who came to Sambalpur in 1766[9] for diamond business, Leckie[9a] who came from Cuttack to Sonepur in 1790 and some other British officials with their parties have moved on this route. *Vividha-Siksha*[10], a Sonepur Durbar publication mentions about the Jagannath Road that starts from Chhatisgarh and ends in Jagannath Puri en route Sambalpur-Sonepur-Boudh-Harbhanga and Cuttack along the right bank of the Mahanadi. Bales of cotton were exported every year through the road and thus giving it another name Cotton Road.

We are further informed[11] that three land routes were passing through Sambalpur. Communication with the coastal part of Odisha was through the Mahanadi river. Salt and other necessities were brought and then transshipped to Raipur, Nagpur and other parts of central India. The land route which connected the coastal area with Raipur passed through Sambalpur. The third route went from Sambalpur to Ranchi, Singhbhum and Calcutta.

Despite of being a hinterland of the country. Sambalpur appears to have been fairly well known to other parts of the country and Europe for its diamond deposits in the beds of the Mahanadi and its tributary the Ib. The best known locality was Hirakud (21^{0}32′ N. Lat; 83^{0}56′ E. Long) near Sambalpur. T. Mothe[11a] was sent on an embassy to Sambalpur in 1766 by Lord Clive. He could not stay long because of the disturbed political state but purchased a few pieces. Lieutenant Kittoe[12] has mentioned about diamonds during his journey in Orissa in 1838. Major Ousley[13] has mentioned about *Hira Khoond*, literally the island of diamonds, near Sambalpur and the procurement of diamond up to Sonepur in his Tour Diary of 1840. Local traditions prevail regarding the find of a large piece during Maratha occupation and the last ruler having another piece. *The Central provinces Gazetteer*[14] informs that some 15 or 20 villages, granted rent-free to *Jhara* people, a professional caste collecting diamond and gold-crust from the rivers, were resumed by the British Government in 1850. Thus Sambalpur had already made a place in the Geological map of India.

Forests

The Tract had, once forest spread over about 4,000 sq. kms lying within the 'great *sal* belt' with varieties of plants like *sal* (*shorea robusta*), *bijassal* (*Pterocarpus marsuipium*), *dhaura* (*anogeissus latifolia*), *arjun* (*terminalia arjuna*), *Karla* (*cleisthanthus collinus*), *kendu* (*diospyrus melanoxylen*), bamboos (*dendrocalamus strectus*), teak (*tectona grandis*), *shisu* or rose wood *dalbergia latifolia*), *gambhari* (*gmelina arborea*), *harda* (*terminalia chebula*), *bahera* (*termenalia belorica*), *kusum* (*schbichera trijuga*) etc. Among principal creepers is *sailppatta* (*bauhinia vahlii*) whose creeper-stem is used for tying heavy things and leaves for making pots. The rebels are said to have tied boulders with the creeper on the sides of hills and cut it to fall down on the British army or on the passage as the case might be.

The Tract is described as a 'paradise' of hunters' by F.C. King in his Sambalpur Gazetteer (1932). He has quoted Mr. Dewar's, who had done the settlement of Sambalpur in 1902-6, statement:

> Sambalpur is reputedly a good big game district, and in past years has been one of the happiest hunting grounds in the Central Provinces. But the cutting out of the forests and the spread of rice and cane cultivation .... Of late years curtailed the grazing ground of wild animals.

King's Gazetteer further says:

> In spite, however, of this diminution in the number of wild animals, and especially of ruminants, few districts in Bihar and Orissa have such a wealth and variety of animal life.

The hill ranges, the rivers and the forests covering the length and breadth of the Sambalpur Tract made it a comparatively isolated part of the Central-Eastern India. Invulnerable, impassable, inhospitable, lacking connectivity with outside regions of the country and importantly, surrounded by Native or Feudatory States, under the suzerainty of the British Indian Empire – Gangpur (Sundargarh) on the north, Patana, Sonepur and Baudh on the south, Bamanda on the east and Raigairh and Sarangarh (both in Chhatisgarh State now) on the west, broadly speaking, it remained a hinterland of the country. Despite the fact that the Tract has a chequered history of its own as a part of South Koshal from Epical time down to that of the illustrious rule of the Somavaṁśīs (cir. A.D. 850-1100). However, the history has been lost in comparative obscurity following 1100 A.D. till the rise of the Chauhanas towards the closing part of 16th century A.D.

HISTORICAL ANTECEDENTS

Sambalpur kingdom came into being as an offshoot of the Chauhan kingdom of Patana under a collateral member named Balaram Deva of the dynasty towards the closing part of 16th century A.D. The establishment of the kingdom was a landmark in the history of not only West Odisha or Odisha but in Central-Eastern India. It played a very vital role in the political developments of West Odisha and adjacent parts of Chhatisgarh from its inception till its conquest and occupation by the British in 1817. Resistance and revolts against the British and their puppet regimes became the order of the day, though they were sporadic and suppressed from 1817 till the annexation to British Indian Empire, by application of Doctrine of Lapse, in 1849.

Sambalpur Tract, under the British Empire, played a very significant role against the British, as said earlier, right from its occupation. The annexation aggravated and worsened the situation to such an extent that the Tract came under the conflagration of

1857 Mutiny which continued with full vigour for five years, i.e., up to 1862 while it was suppressed elsewhere in other parts of the country in a year or two.   It is significant to note in the context that the majority of the people were tribals who were illiterate and poor, they did not have any organization or requisite weaponry to fight against the British Imperial Power. Yet they carried it on for five years through untold hardships, sufferings and privation. Rarely history of the region has witnessed such acts of bravery and courage, some rare feats of sufferings and sacrifice for the cause of the Tract.

The modi operandi for fighting against the British, the nature of a prolonged rebellion and, most importantly, the people who had monitored the activities have remained unresearched for a long time. Of late, the roles of the *Zamindars* and the people have been coming to light. In fact, the *Zamindari*s created by the Chauhana rulers played a crucial role which accounts for the occurrence and continuation of the Mutiny in the Tract.

Land Tenure Systems : Khalsa

For a precise understanding of the support of *Zamindars* to the Rebellion of 1857 for a long time and in a wholehearted manner, we have to go deep into the existing nature of land tenure system which the British Government wanted to abolish or replace with their own arrangement. Before British annexation of Sambalpur in 1849 Sambalpur kingdom was broadly divided into two kinds of land systems, viz., *Khalsa* and *Zamindari*. The former included all sorts of land held by the King or State Government directly. It had covered 1,657 sq. miles and consisted of 119 *malguzari*,

870 *gaunti* and 16 *ryotwari* villages. There were five classes of proprietors in the *Khalsa*, viz., the *Gauntia*, the *Malguzar*, the *Bhogra Bhogi*, the *Malik Makbuza* and *Brahmattar*.

The *Gauntias* (village headmen) were described as the most predominant and a peculiar class of proprietors. They were responsible for collection and payment of revenue for the village to the king for a period 'according to a lease which was periodically revised and renewed'. For his services, the *Gauntia* was remunerated with undisturbed enjoyment of home-farm i.e. *bhogra* land free of rent or 25 percent of total revenue of the ryots. If rental value of home farm became more than that he had to pay, the excess was considered as *zapti* and, if less, he was given *puraskar* to the extent of loss. They were rarely ejected for default of payment, in such case they paid *nazrana* (an imposed fee) from their earning and continued to retain the *gaunti*, because it was "not only a source of income, but also it meant a great social prestige which he could never afford to loose"[15]. He was 'a trustee' on behalf of the State.

The *Malguzars* of Sambalpur were 'full proprietors in villages held by them'. L.S.S. O'Malley has observed that they held estates 'revenue-free or paid only nominal quit-rents'. Often, they paid less than the *Gauntia*.

The *Bhogra-Bhogis* enjoyed unimpeded proprietary right over small parcels of land of a village. They did not pay any rent to the village assessment except sometimes *Zapti* or excess assessment when the rental value of their land exceed 25 percent of ryoti rental of the village.

Malik makbuza was the same as *Bhogra-Bhogi* lands held by Malguzars, although there are a few such when *Bhogra-Bhogi* lands were many. This tenure has been referred to be 13 in the District Gazetteer of F.C. King.

Brahmottar or *Devototar* lands consisted of plots granted rent-free and in perpetuity to Brahmins and temples. Such lands were too many in the district, created for the maintenance of temples and socio-religious services of the Brahmins.

Creation of Zamindaris in Sambalpur Tract

The political and administrative history of Sambalpur Kingdom, it is rightly said, 'can be hardly dealt in isolation of the numerous territorial and administrative changes that it had undergone during the last one and half centuries'[16] i.e. from 1817 when the British Government occupied Sambalpur after defeating the Marathas in the Anglo-Maratha War. Properly speaking, creation of various kinds of fiefs – *Zamindaris, maufidaris, Thekadaris* – generally known as *Zamindaris* had been created at different times by rulers, since the establishment of Chauhana Kingdom in the later phase of 16th century A.D. to meet political and filial needs. By the time of outbreak of the Mutiny, thus there were sixteen *Zamindari*s. In fact, the territorial units created by the kings of Sambalpur played a vital role in the body-politics of the State or Tract.

For sometime, the dominion of the king of Sambalpur extended beyond the traditional or natural frontiers of the kingdom.. Whereas during the first ruler Balalram Dev's reign (1580-1600 A.D), Bamanda (Deograrh District), Gangpur (Sundargarh District), Surguja (Chhatisgarh) were compelled to accept the suzerainty of Sambalpur after their defeats, in the reign of Baliar Dev (1650-90), as many as eighteen Kingdoms (*athara-garhs*) both in Orissa and Chhatisgarh accepted the paramountcy of Sambalpur. However, the status of the feudatories vis-à-vis the paramount king – whether limited to some regular payments and supply of armed forces or acceptance of nominal vassalage – is not precisely known. Some of them behaved like feudal lords who, of course, can not be termed as *Zamindar* which has a different connotation in the context of the Tract as discussed in the following pages.

It appears that the *Zamindaris* were created from the time of fourth ruler Madhukakra Dev (1630-50 A.D) to appease and accommodate his sons. The Sambalpur throne was the reserve of the eldest, Baliar, according to the time – honoured tradition of law of primogeniture. Whereas the newly conquered area of Sonepur from the king of Sonepur-Baudh was made a separate kingdom under his second son Madan Gopal Dev, Rajpur-Khinda was organized as *maufidari* estate (popularly called *Zamindari*) and, was bestowed on his third son Aniruddh. The fourth and youngest son Vamsi Gopal became a renunciant, he was not a claimant of any estate probably.

However, in literature of later time, e.g., in *Sambala Manasa*[17] by Svapneshvar Dash, Rajpur has been described as a *Zamindari* and Khinda as a *Maufidari*.

Baliar Dev (1650-89) created two *Zamindaris*, namely, Barpali and Saria and appointed his two younger sons Vikram Singh and Fatal Singh respectively on them. He also awarded a *Gond* Sardar named Uddam with a *Zamindari* named Kharsal. A descendant of Uddam named Dial Sardar was hanged in 1858 for participation in the rebellion of Surendra Sai. Among the *maufidaris*, mention may be made of Huma, a village on the bank of the Mahanadi near Sambalpur and conferred on a Brahmin for maintenance of worship of the Siva temple there[18]. Chhatra Sai (1691-1725), the grandson of Baliar bestowed Rampur *Zamindari* on Pran Nath Rajput who helped him to get the throne of Sambalpur after suppressing a rebellion in Sambalpur in 1690. His son Ajit Singh (1725-66) set up a village named after him as Ajitapura Sasan (present Sasan on Sambalpur-Jharsuguda road). His *Dewan* Dakshnina Raya set up the Kedarnath Siva temple at Ambabhana in present Bargarh district and gave two villages named Talpali and Satidara as *muafi* for maintenance of the temple. Jayant Singh (1781-1818) created two *Maufi* villages named Jayantapur and Themra. Two copper plates[19] of his reign have been discovered, which record the donation of two villages named Themra and Sudunga near Sambalpur.

Kolabira *Zamindari* was created in the reign of Jayant Singh (781-1818). Its *Zamindar* took an active part in the rebellion of Surendra Sai and was hanged, while his son died as an outlaw declared by the British Government. The *Zamindar* was *Gond* by caste. Kudabaga, Loisingha, Bheren, Kharsal, Loida, Pahjadsirgida etc. had *Gond Zamindars* while Ghens and Borasambar (Padampur) of Bargarh disitrict) were under *Binjhal* tribe *Zamindars*. The *Zamindaris* were divided into two groups, viz., *Dandapata* (big *Zamindaris*) and *Gadti* (small *Zamindaris*). Six of the *Dandapatas* viz. Bijepur, Ghens, Patkulunda, Bheden, Kharsal (Kankvira) and Pahad Sirgida are known as *dakshina-tira* (i.e. located on the south), now in Bargarh district, seven, viz., Kolabira, Rampur, Rajpur, Kudabaga, Machida, Loisingha and Loida were known as *Uttara-tira* (i.e. located on the north) in Sambalpur and Jharsuguda districts[20].

Zamindaris : Salient Features

The *Zamindaris,* on the other hand, were 'tracts held by proprietors having feudal status'. The Sambalpur Gazetteer[21] has described:

> The *Zamindar* in Sambalpur was an ordinary proprietor who paid, instead of a *Kamil jama* of full assessment a feudal *takoli* or tribute which was invariably much less than a full proprietary assessment.

> The *Zamindar* of Sambalpur occupied a position which was mid-way between the Chief of a Feudatory State who paid tribute to the British Government, and the ordinary proprietor of *Khalsa* village, who used to pay a portion of his assets as land revenue. The tenure of the *Zamindar* was not laid down in any Act, but it was expressed in the *Wazib-ul-urz* or village administration record, accepted by him on each Settlement. Whenever the terms and conditions embodied in the *Wazib-ul-urz* appeared to be doubtful or vague, definite orders of the Government used to be issued amplifying a dubious point or interpreting apparently confusing provisions. Briefly, the legal status of the *Zamindars* was that they were proprietors of the estates which were impartible and non-transferable except to heirs, who too had to be approved by the Government. Each estate was held by the *Zamindar* only on specified terms, and he could be theoretically dispossessed in case of continued gross mismanagement of the estate or willful violation of the terms embodied in the *Wazib-ul-urz*. The rights and privileges of the *Zamindars* were personal and a condition was imposed in the *Wazib-ul-urz*, that should at any time the estate be transferred otherwise than in accordance with the procedure mentioned in the *Wazib-ul-urz*, the Government would be at liberty to impose full land revenue and forest assessment and to resume all special *Zamindari* privileges. These *Zamindaris* were, therefore comparable to permanently settled estates of Bengal with certain restrictions. Here it may be recalled that no permanent dispossession of *Zamindari* did actually occur in Sambalpur, even after may of them rose in revolt against the British Government in 1857. On the other hand, the right of the Government to determine succession was rigidly enforced, and the impartibility of the estate had been

insisted upon. No person other than the *Zamindar* had been recognized as proprietor of land within a *Zamindari* or had successfully contested his claim to proprietorship.

It has further described:

> The revenue history of the *Zamindaris* goes back to ancient times when *Gonds* and *Bhinjals* were the ruling Chiefs of Sambalpur. But whatever their origin may have been, it appears that before the district (Sambalpur) came under direct British administration, (in 1849) while it was under the rule of the Rajas of Sambalpur, the *Zamindaris* were service tenures held on payment of a small tribute called *Takoli* subject to the condition that the proprietors were bound to render military service when required. When the district escheated to the British, these *Zamindars* who held in perpetuity continued in the enjoyment of their tenures on payment of their existing *Takoli* and were directed to perform police duties instead of rendering military service. During the Rebellion of Surendra Sai from 1857 to 1862 nine of the 16 *Zamindaris*, namely, Kolabira, Kudabaga, Ghens, Pahadsirgida, Patkulunda, Rampur, Bheran, Kharsal and Mandomahal were confiscated in consequence of their proprietors having joined in the Revolt, but later on, they were restored to their respective proprietors on the eve of proclamation of amnesty in 1859.

Maufidars : Features and Difference from Zamindaris

Some other designations of feudal land holders like *Maufidar* and *Thekadar*, though a little different from the status of *Zamindar*, were also commonly known or addressed as *Zamindars*. Of course, *Zamindar* was a more popular term which included the two varieties in its ambit and some of them like the *Maufidiar* of Rajpur has been taken as a *Zamindar* in the context of the present investigation.

In the case of *Maufidari* it has been explained as:

> In the *Zamindaris* many villages were held free of rent by persons who were either relations of the *Zamindars* or his former servants. They were commonly known as *Maufidars*.

The *Maufi* was against the *Zamindar* and not against the Government. Therefore the *Maufidars* used to pay proportionate share of land revenue payable by the *Zamindar* to Government. This is, however, an amicable arrangement which had no official recognition. *Maufidars* agitated to have absolute right in the villages held by them. But as they were creations of the *Zamindar*, their true status was something intermediate between the tenant and the *Zamindar*. The only peculiar feature in the incidences of the *Maufidars'* right was that they held their villages rent-free[22].

Among other *Maufidaris* (free-hold tenures) mention may be made of Roshada, Bargarh, Godbhaga, Jharsuguda, Tampargarh, Kirttipura, Chakuli etc. S Dash[23] has informed us that the first one was conferred on Babu Banamali Khansama who had got as many as 18 *maufi vrittis* i.e. eighteen *garha* while Balki Dash, grandfather of S. Dash, who has been killed in action by the *Gond* rebels led by Bandya Ray and Mahapatra Ray. The grant (*maufi*) given to the sons of Balki Dash by king Narayan Singh is known as *Sirkata* (given for getting beheaded). We are informed that 167 villages[24] were held as free-hold tenures which were held by members of the royal family, Brahmins for maintenance of temples, royal servants and *Inamdars*. Sometimes individuals were also conferred villages as free-gifts in perpetuity. Such 45 villages (10 *maujas* and 35 *Dakhlees*) were granted on payment of a nominal rent. The late Rajas have granted 15 villages (3 *maujas* and 12 *Dakhlees*) to Babu Ojjal Singh and his brothers – brothers of Surendra Sai who participated in the Rebellion of 1857.

Thekadar

The *Thekadar*[25] held an intermediate position between the tenants and the *Zamindar* in the *Zamindari* system. His duty was to collect revenue from the people and pay the *Thekajama* to *Zamindar.* He was given home-farm land (*sir*) in the village for his services. On renewal of *theka* (lease*), he had to* pay *nazrana to Zamindars.* Many of the aboriginal *thekadars* failed to compete with the rich Hindu men who came to stake bid and, were ousted. Further, though home-farm land was forbidden for partition, it was divided among members of *thekadar's* family and that frequently led to quarrels, which made the tenants to suffer from unnecessary litigation. All that created a lot of resentment among both the *thekadar* and the people.

Zamindari and Tribes

A precise account of the existence of *Zamindari*s in Sambalpur Tract before the foundation of the Chauhan rule in the closing part of 16th century A.D. is not available to us. In fact, the political condition of the Tract of that time is somewhat hazy. Very likely, the tribal chieftains – most of whom were of the *Gond* tribe, divided the area into some estates and, each one exercised his power and authority on the people in it. The influence of the *Gond Zamindars* of such *Zamindari*s like Kolabira, Pahadsirgida, Machida, Kudobaga, Loida, Loisingha, Mundomahal and Lakhanpur was prevalent before the advent of the Chauhanas.

The establishment of the Chauhan rule came as a bit of shock to the *Zamindars* or tribal chieftains. They were taken aback. Before they could organize themselves for any opposition or start resistance against the newly founded rule, the founder of Chauhan rule Balaram Dev realized the situation and started doing the needful to placate and appease them.

It may be pointed out in the context that of the forty or a little more of the number of tribes the *Gonds,* the *Binjhals,* the *Mirdhas,* the *Sahra* etc. were quite numerous and influential. 'The *Gonds* are most influential of all the Dravidian tribes'. They migrated from *Gond*wana (present Madhya Pradesh) and established their rule in various parts of that country during 13th-14th centuries A.D. In course of time, some of them migrated to adjacent land of West Odisha and 'severed connection with their overlords in Madhya Pradesh'. Some powerful ones of them established their estates and ruled like kings. They also started marital relation with other chiefs and kings of West Odisha and Madhya Pradesh-Chhatisgarh region.

The Sambalpur District Gazetteer records a tradition as follows:[26]

> The sway of the *Gond* rulers was light and the agricultural prosperity of the country increased under them, and works, like the great reservoir Rani Talao near Jubbelpore, remain to this day as monuments of their rule. An excellent practice of the *Gond* kings was to give anyone who made a tank a grant of revenue free land lying below it. This tradition was maintained during the *Gond* rule in Sambalpur under which certain remissions of revenue were granted for construction of tanks and other agricultural improvements.

Balaram Dev, the king of Sambalpur must have realized that besides being a claimant to royal pedigree, they were numerous, influential, hard-working and, importantly, trustworthy and loyal. Further, he must be in need of recruits to the army, chieftains to take care of smaller revenue-administrative units for maintenance of law and order and collection of revenue. So he started pleasing them by conferring the status of the old fief-holders and creating a few new ones. He respected their sentiments as well by honouring their time-honoured religious practices. Some of their deities were accepted as the royal numen. Thus they were coming closer and closer towards the 'nuclear areas' of the body-politic of the State. He gave a purpose and a direction to his successors who followed it. It paid dividends. They accepted the suzerainty of the king. In fact, they became a prop, a pillar of strength to the kings in times of both war and peace. It was with their help that Baliar Dev, the fifth ruler (1650-90 A.D) established his suzerainty over eighteen kingdoms (*athara gada*). The tribal *Zamindars* performed an important role during the coronation ceremony of the kings. In fact – power, strength and successes of the kings depended upon the whole-hearted support and loyalty of the tribals *Zamindars* to a large extent.

Similarly, the other important tribe *Binjhal* 'appear to have been among the earliest inhabitants of the district (Sambalpur)'. They trace their original abode to Ratanpur (Bilaspur district) of Chhatisgarh. A prevalent tradition[27] says that the founder of the Chauhan rule of West Odisha Ramai Dev at Patanagarh (Balangir district) cir. 1350-80 A.D. was born in the house of a *Beriha* (a title borne by small hilly land chiefs of *Binjhal* tribe) when his mother a Rajput princess was running away from Mainpuri (Agra, Uttar Pradesh) after her husband was slain in a battle by the Muslims. Like the *Gonds* in Sambalpur, the *Binjhal* chief of Borasambar, the biggest of *Zamindaris*, tie the royal *saree* on the head of the king of Patana State during coronation. Ghens *Zamindari* was also under a *Binjhal* chief. These *Zamindaris* have made supreme sacrifices for the cause of the Tract against the British during the Rebellion of 1857. Those have become legendary and have a few parallels in the annals of history.

Political Condition on the Eve of the British Occupation

The power and glory of Sambalpur kingdom were in tact till the time of Chhatra Sai (1691-1725), the seventh ruler. The traditional subordinate territories, *athara-gada, tera dandapata* (eighteen fortresses and thirteen fiscal divisions) were in existence. The *Zamindars* were quiet and loyal. No incident of any unpleasant kind was heard in any part of the *Zamindari*s. T. Mottee, who visited Sambalpur in 1766 in the reign of Ajit Singh (1725-66), has noted that "the inhabitants therein (Sambalpur) must be leading a life, one of comfort and contentment".

The observation of R.K. Mishra[28] gives a clear piciture of the relation between Sambalpur kingdom and the *Zamindari*s and Feudatory states.

> Kolabira, Ghess, Lakhanpur, Ambabana, Bhukta and many other *garhotteas* (*Zamindar*s) were coming under the category of autonomous unit having their own militia and responsible for defending the Confederacy and extending loyalty to the overlordship of Sambalpur. So strong was this bond between Sambalpur and the Confederated States that Goddess Samaleswari, the presiding deity of Sambalpur, was venerated as the central figure.

However, things started tking an adverse turn in the reign of Ajit Singh (1725-66). A. Dash[29] has put it as:

> Towards the later part of the regime of Ajit Singh, the seed of anarchy was sown and it was a breeding ground for disruption, dissention and internal feud leading to a sense of insecurity and uncertainty of life and properties, economical and moral degradation of the people and gradual weakness of the sovereign power.

T. Mottee also gives an account of the maladministration in Sambalpur during 1763-66. The king became a puppet in the hands of his Dewans.

The mission of T. Mottee who was sent by Robert Clive was to open a trade in diamonds but he was instructed "to get a first hand information of the condition of Sambalpur, pave the way for the subsequent operation of the Britishers to establish themselves and rule over the territory of diamonds"[30]. However, on May 30, 1766 night due to a stroke of lightning, he lost some 16 men, he left Sambalpur in hot-haste condemning the place all through his narrative. His mission of buying Sambalpur from the Marathas through peaceful negotiations and starting a mining trade and securing money for remittance to England 'did not progress even one step further'. A. Dash[31] has remarked:

> It can not, however be doubted that the seed of anarchy had been shown in Sambalpur during the last days of Raja Ajit Singh, which facilitated the staging of a political rebellion headed by Surendra Sai for native rule in Sambalpur and its consequential repression by the Britishers for long years.
>
> The political activities of Surendra Sai to achieve his objective had three-fold consequences on the people, viz., the attempt of the Britishers to establish themselves in Sambalpur through the puppet Raja Narayan Singh (1833-49), the widespread rebellion of Surendra Sai with the help of influential people and some *Zamindars* and the secret help of some *Rajas* to frustrate the attempt of the Britishers and the consequent miseries of the common people to survive in the midst of this conflict between these two powerful forces.

Ajit Singh's death (1766 A.D) brought in chaotic condition in Sambalpur kingdom. His son Abhay Singh (1766-78) became a puppet in the hands of the powerful *Dewan* Akbar Ray. In the reign of Ajit, the Bhonsala of Nagpur Raghuji I (1738-55) had occupied Cuttack Province from the Bengal Nawab Alivarivardi Khan in 1751. Since Sambalpur became a buffer region between Cuttack and Nagpur and, secondly, the

Bhonsala dared not attack the hilly land Sambalpur, he made friendship and gave valuable presents to Ajit Singh for getting a passage through Sambalpur. However, he planned to capture Sambalpur since it was a necessity for maintaining the Maratha hold over Cuttack. In the reign of Januji Bhonsala (1755-72) Babu Khan, a general of Bhonsla, attacked Sambalpur but was repulsed by Akbar Ray[32], Dewan of Sambalpur. The combined revolt of the Kodabaga and Khinda *Zamindars* against the reign of terror of Akbar Ray was suppressed by the latter[33].

Conquest of Sambalpur was a very difficult job for the Marathas. The British correspondence records:

> Sambalpur was the principal fortress of a Chief of Mountaineers x x x x an extensive tract of country between Chhatisgarh (i.e. Ruttunpur and Cuttack x x x x Governing a numerous tribe of hardy mountaineers and possessing such a stronghold as Sambalpur, he had been hitherto able to elude the power of the Raja of Berar and all attempts to subdue his country had been invariably failed[34].

However, conquest of Sambalpur by Marathas could not brook any delay. Raghuji II (1775-88) perturbed the Sambalpur king by repeated incursions and the latter Jayant Singh (1781-1818) at last agreed to pay *Chauth* by a settlement made in 1794 (Samvat 1850)[35]. That arrangement could not last long on the alibi of Sambalpur Dewan's failure to attend the Bhonsale who was passing through Sambalpur for Puri in 1799. In a surprise attack king Jayant Singh and his son Maharaj Sai were taken as captives to Chanda (Maharastra) where they stayed till 1817. Coolbrooke, Resident at Nagpur became perturbed at the developments and reported the matter to Governor-General Wellesley[36].

After defeat in the Second Anglo-Maratha War, according to Treaty of Deogaon on December 17, 1803, the British occupied Provinces of Cuttack. However, their attempts to capture "feudatories of *Senah Saheb Sobah*" (Raja of Nagpur) by hook or crook, have failed. It has been pointed out:

> The *Zamindars*, from long and painful experience, have acquired so thorough distrust in and bitter aversion to the Maratha Government that no appearances however plausible, or assurances however sincere would again induce them to place confidence in or be reconciled to their former sovereign[37].

Wellesley's ratification of the Treaty on January 9, 1804[38] and his ultimatum to Marathas worked and Sambalpur came under the British control.

However, the East India Company's authorities in England did not like Wellesley's policy of War and annexation. His successor G.H. Barlow restored Sambalpur and Patna kingdoms to Marathas in 1806. The Marathas were defeated decisively in the third Anglo-Maratha war at Sitalbad on November 17,1817. Thereafter the whole of West Orissa came under the British control.

The *Zamindars* did not play any role or rather they had no role in the drama of Maratha and then British occupation during 1799 to 1817. They had tacit support to the Queen Ratan Kumari when she had stood against the Marathas. The reason was there was little interference in the affairs of *Zamindaris*. The Marthas were only concerned with collection of *Chauth*. Sometimes the Maratha soldiers entered into the inaccessible areas of *Zamindar*ies for any exactions.

References

1.   Senapati, N. (ed) : *Orissa District Gazetteers Sambalpur,* (hereinafter referred to as *Sambalpur*), Bhubaneswar, 1971, pp. 348-9.

2.   *ibid,* pp. 348-9.

3.   *ibid,* pp. 348-9.

4.   Mishra, R.K. : *Surendra Sai Pioneer of a Complete Revolution,* Sambalpur, 2002 (hereinafter referred to as *Surendra Sai,* 2002), p. 57.

5.   *Sambalpur,* 1971, p. 11.

6.   *Orissa Historical Research Journal* (hereinafter referred as *OHRJ*), Bhubaneswar, 1999, XLIII, Nos. 1-4, pp. 107-13.

7.   *OHRJ,* IV, Nos. 3-4, p. 47.

8.   *Early European Travelers in Nagpur Territories,* Government Press, Nagpur, 1930.

9.   *Asiatic Annual Register,* London, 1799. A Narrative of a Journey to the Diamond Mines at Sambalpur in the Province of Orissa.

9a.   *OHRJ,* XLIII, Nos. 1-4, p. 111.

10.   Mallik, S.C. : *Vividha Siksha,* Sonepur, 1910, pp. 19-21.

11.   *Surendra Sai,* 2002, pp. 59-60.

11a.   Asiatic Annual Register, op. cit.

12.   *JASB,* VIII, 1839, p. 375.

13.   *ibid,* p. 1057.

14.   *Sambalpur, 1971,* p. 87 (quoted).

15.   *ibid,* p. 346.

16.   *ibid,* p. 344.

17.   Dash, Svapneshwar : *Sambala Manasā* (Oriya), Sambalpur, 1923, pp. 16-20 (hereinafter referred to as *Manasā*)

18.   *ibid.*

19.   Dash, Siva Prasad   : *Sambalpur Itihāsa* (Oriya), 2nd Edn., Sambalpur, 1968 (hereinafter referred to as *Itihāsa*), 1968, pp. 469-70.

20.   *Manasa,* p. 16, *Itihasa,* p. 464.

20a.   *Sambalpur,* p. 349.

21.   *Sambalpur, 1971*, pp. 348-9.

22.   *ibid,* pp. 351-52.

23.   *Manasā*, pp. 16-20.

24.   *Surendra Sai, 2002*, p. 54.

25.   *Sambalpur, 1971*, p. 352.

26.   *ibid,* p. 117.

27.   Impey, H.B : "*Notes on Gurhjat State of Patna*", OHRJ, 111, No. 2;   Grant, Charles : *Gazetteers of Central Provinces of India*, 1909, pp. 393-34; O,Malley : *Bengal Districts Gazetteers Sambalpur*, 1909, p. 21;   Cobden-Ramsay, L.C.P. : *Feudatory State of Orissa*, p. 284.

28.   Surendra Sai, 2002*, p. 66.*

29.   Dash, A ̈*Life of Surendra Sai*, Cuttack, 1963, p. 14 (hereinafter refrerred to as *Life, 1963).*

30.   *ibid, p. 20.*

31.   *ibid,* pp. 18-19.

32.   *Itihasa, 1968*, p. 181.

33.   *Paṇḍulipi* (Oriya) by Satyavadi Mishra.

34.   Selections from Nagpur Residency Records, (hereinafter referred to as *Selections*), Vol. I, 34.   (Letter from H. Colebrooke, Resident at Nagpur to Right Hon'ble Earl of Mornington, Governor-General, dated nil April 1800).

35.	*ibid,* p. 54.	(Letter
fro m E.S. Broughton to N.B. Edmonstone, Secretary to Government, April 2,
1804).

36.	*Selections,* p. 34.

37.	*ibid,* p. 52.

38.	Aitchinson, C.U. : A Collecltion of Treaties, Engagements and Sanads Relating to
India and Neighbouring Countries, III, Calcutta, 1929-31. (hdereinafter referred
to as *Collelction*).

CHAPTER 2

THE *ZAMINDARIS*

A PRELUDE TO 1857 MUTINY

The four decades (1817-57) preceding to the 1857 Mutiny, that is, from the occupation of Sambalpur by the British to the annexation to the British Indian Empire in 1849 and the following 8 years, is a period of chaos, anarchy and maladministration for the Sambalpur Tract and, revolts and lawlessness in the *Zamindaris*. Those continued unabated till the fire of the Mutiny rose high in its flames, spread like a wild fire among various parts of Sambalpur Tract and, continued with vigour for full five years (1857-62) having witnessed chivalry, dauntless fighting against the mighty British Imperial Power and exemplary sacrifices for the cause of the motherland. The Tract, considered to be a hinterland of the country, continued fighting against the British for five years, when it has been suppressed elsewhere in the country. Some of the *Zamindars* and the people played such significant roles that are fit to be recorded in the annals of fight for freedom of the country.

Maharaja Jayant Singh of Sambalpur was released from Maratha captivity in 1817 and made ruler of Sambalpur. He died a little time after in 1818. His son Maharaja Sai was a minor and administration was run by Political Agent Roughsedge.

It was kept under the jurisdiction of Sout-West Frontier Agency. Maharaja Sai was made king in 1820 with restricted powers, i.e. without paramountcy over feudatories of Sambalpur He was given *Zamindari* tenure of *Khalsa* villages at an annual rent by a *Sanad* for 5 years (1821-26). Thus the British became de facto authority and the king a mere figure head. Hardly a year after renewal of *Sanad* in 1827 Maharaja Sai died without leaving behind a heir to the throne.

Mohan Kumari (1827-33)

The year 1827 marks a turning pointing the history of Sambalpur kingdom. A sort of chaotic condition came to prevail in the kingdom. There came out a number of claimants to the throne. But of those, four had rights. The first of them was Ranajit Singh, a great grandson of Chhatra Sai (1691-1725) the seventh ruler of Sambalpur Chauhana dynasty. He was also a favourite of Maharaja Sai, as revealed from a letter of Deputy Commissioner Cumberledge dated July 21, 1866, and he expected that the throne would come to him. However, his claim was set aside for the queen of Maharaja Sai, Mohan Kumari who was installed on the throne. The queen created a *maufi* in Jharsuguda for Ranjit. Ranjit accepted the fait accompli and remained quiet for sometime. His son Govind, however, was discontented and raised a standard of revolt at Chandrapur (Chhatisgarh) against the queen. He was supported by Thakur Ajit Singh of Bargarh. However, Govind was defeated and taken as a captive. After the death of the last king Narayan Singh (1833-49) of Sambalpur, Govind was made the Chief or *maufidar* of Jharsuguda. The *muafi* was made permanent in 1867 by the British.

The second claimant was *Zamindar* of Barpali, Bhavani Singh – a descendant of Vikram Singh, the son of Baliar Dev of Sambalpur (1650-89). The third claimant was Raja Prithvi Singh of Sonepur (1786-1841), a descendent of Madan Gopal, second son Madhukar Sai (1630-50), the 4th king of Sambalpur. The fourth was Balaram Sai, the *maufidar* of Khinda, the son of– Anniruddha who was the son of king Madhukar Sai of Sambalpur .

It may be pointed out in the context that Balaram Sai was instrumental in the installation of Rani Mohan Kumari on the throne of Sambalpur. He became the *Dewan*. Balaram appears to have persuaded the queen to create Jharsuguda *mauafidari* and, thus removing Ranjit Singh from staking a claim to the throne of Sambalpur. Prithvi Singh, the king of Sonepur was in the captivity of the Marathas for a long period. After his release, continuance of the succession in Sonepur became more important since his only son Raghunath had died when he (Prithvi Singh) was in captivity. Bhavani Singh (of Barpali) though a young man, with an infant son was persuaded by some people for a contest to the throne of Sambalpur. He was, however, not much interested. Thus, Balaram hoped that the wind would blow in his favour after a few years' rule of the queen.

Things, however, took a different turn. Ranjit Singh of Jharsuguda rose in revolt for the throne of Sambalpur for sometime. The queen got him arrested and kept him in detention at Sambalpur. His son Govind, as told earlier, raised a standard of revolt. Cap Wilkinson and Lt. Higgins suppressed the revolt with great difficulty. However, Ranjit and Govind were pardoned and Jharsuguda was restored to them.

In the mean time, Rani Mohan Kumari was deposed from the throne in 1833 and sent off to Cuttack on a pension[1]. She was weak but an opportunist. She deprived the tribal *Zamindars* of their traditional rights and privileges at the instance of the British. She even revoked the grants of land made to them by Ratna Kumari, queen of Jayat Singh for their help against the Marathas. The British Government picked up Narayan Singh, the old aged uncle of Bhavani Singh, the *Zamindar* of Barpali and made him the king of Sambalpur on October 11, 1833. The hope of Balaram Sai of Khinda was razed to the ground.

Balaram Sai adopted a new tactics to obtain the throne of Sambalpur. He started organizing the discontented tribal people in general and their chieftains in particular against the British Government. The importance of the tribal *Zamindars* was reduced to almost nil after the British Government chose Mohan Kumari and then Narayan Singh as rulers. The role the *Zamindars* had been playing during the anointment ceremony of the Sambalpur king was thrown to wind. The tribal people were charged with heavy demand of revenue for the land which they had been cultivating free of rent or at a nominal rent. Not only the tribal people but also the general people were also feeling resentful at the exorbitant revenue demand. It is observed:

> After the death of Raja Narayuan Singh in 1849 when the Tract escheated to the British Government, a hasty revenue settlement appears to have been made only to be followed by a second one in 1854. These settlements were rather perfunctory in nature and there were considerable shortcomings in the operations. No papers about these settlements are at present traceable[2].

The people of the Tract could not forget the good old days of which

> there was no detailed record showing the amount of land revenue collected under the native rule, but from the amount of quit rent then fixed on some privileged estates and the tributes paid by feudal *Zamindars* as well as from the customary rent and revenue found payable in the *Khalsa* (royal demesne) and common village in 1864, it is noticed that the revenue annually realized in cash by the Raja of Sambalpur was very small not exceeding probably rupees one lakh[3].

Balaram Sai started fishing in the troubled waters to his advantage. Instead of exposing himself, for fear of being considered as selfish, he appealed the people to come forward in support of his nephew Surendra (Sundar) Sai. The old and imbecile king Narayan Singh became perturbed and decided to act against Balaram Sai and his co-rebels. Instead of exposing himself, for fear of being considered as selfish, he appealed the people to come forward in support of his nephew Surendra (Sundar) Sai. The old and imbecile king Narayan Singh became perturbed and decided to act against Balaram Sai and his co-rebels.

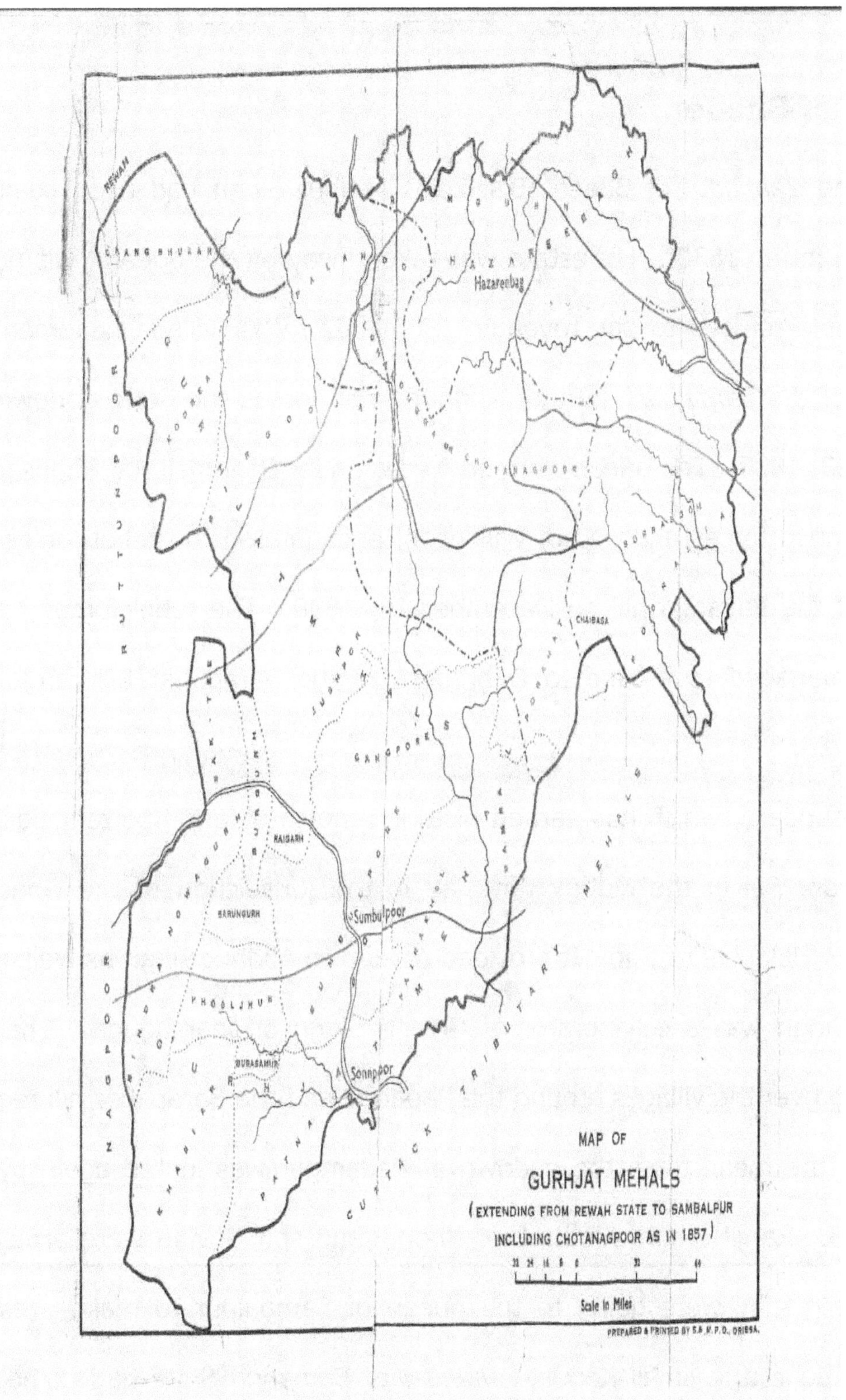
REWAH
CHANGBHUJAR
PALAMOW
HAZAREE
Hazareebag
KOODRA
SIRGOOJA
BUNDO
CHOTANAGPOOR
BORRASOOM
CHAIBASA
RUTTUNPOOR
KORBA
JUSHPOOR
GANGPORE
RAISARH
SARUNGURH
Sumbulpoor
PHOOLJHUR
BURASAMUR
Sonnpoor
CUTTACK TRIBUTARY MEHPO
KOORZ
PATNA
MAP OF
GURHJAT MEHALS
(EXTENDING FROM REWAH STATE TO SAMBALPUR
INCLUDING CHOTANAGPOOR AS IN 1857)
Scale In Miles
PREPARED & PRINTED BY S.A.M.P.O., ORISSA.

Revolt of Bheden

The *Zamindar* of Bheen (Biseikela) Abdhut Singh had risen against the queen Mohan Kumri in 1830[4]. His estate was taken away by the queen. His numerous *Gond* tribe people refused to pay revenue. Some *Gauntias* (village headmen) came out in support of the *Zamindar.* Further Abdhut Singh looted the State godown at Padampur on July 23, 1830. The queen's armed forces under Banamali Rai Khansama, supported by the British forces under Cap. Wilkinson, encountered the rebel forces in the foothill region of the Papanga hill on December 16, 1830. The rebel forces surrendered but Abdhut managed to escape to Debrigarh on the Barapahar hill range in Lakhanpur *Zamindari.*

Debrigarh, which has earned historic renown as an important base of operation of Surendra Sai in the Mutiny time lay in the jurisdiction of the Gond *Zamindar* of Lakhanpur Balabhadra Dao. It provided asylum to Abdhut Singh as well as Balaram Sai. Abdhut Singh was a collaborator of Govind Singh of Jharsuguda. The rebellion was spreading over the villages around the Papanga and the Barapahar hill regions.

In the mean time, the godown at Padampur was looted again by the rebels in July 1833. Ranjit Singh, his brother Bhopal and son Govind were arrested on July 8, 1832 when they were going to the queen of Sambalpur to make presents (*salami*). Chandra Behera, a small Kondh *Zamindar* of Bamanda State had come out openly in support of Govind Singh's claim. He fought a few encounters with the British forces and lost a good number of his fighters. The king of Khariar Krishna Chandra Singh supported the revolt launched by the members of the family of Govind of Jharsuguda against Govind's detention at Sambalpur. The presence of Wilkinson with forces was of no avail and the denial of help to the queen's appeal by such headmen like Medini Rai of Kharmunda and Trilochan Rai of Pahadsirgida etc. further worsened the situation. British forces started coming to Sambalpur.

Wilkinson realized that the situation should not be allowed to deteriorate. He wanted to establish peace through negotiations. He invited Balaram Sai and his associates to come to Lapanga near Jharsuguda for talks. He further promised them to return the estate confiscated by the queen. On March 5, 1831 Abdhut Singh of Bheden, Arjun Singh of Loisingh, Sivanath Rai of Kudabaga-Bareipali etc. were restored to their estates.

Despite Wilkinson's efforts, discontentment continued to prevail. Sometimes, the policy of the queen added fuel to fire of the disturbances. In February 5, 1833, Govind Singh, his associate Chandra Behera, Sikru *Zamindar* appeared in the outskirts of Sambalpur despite the resistance of the British forces. Lt. Higgins could not face the arrows of the rebels and returned to Sambalpur. About 500 people under one Megha Rai and Medini Rai (Chandra Behera's brother) made surprise attacks on the British forces at Dhanupali. However, they were defeated and driven away by the British forces.

Lt. Higgins was attacked when he was going to Hazaribag en route Maneshar. He was forced to return to Sambalpur. Sikru *Zamindar*'s attempt to occupy Sakhi

Gopinath temple of Sambalpur was foiled. The rebel leaders Govind Singh, Chandra Behera and Sikru *Zamindar* had retreated with their respective forces.

Cap. Wilkinson prepared operations against Jagabandhu Babu who had gathered rebels on the Papanga hill. He had left the place with the rebels when the Government forces arrived there. However, he was captured by the Raja of Sonepur. A search operation resulted in the capture of rebel leaders like Arjun Gauntia, Rahu Biswal, Sobhnath *Gond*, Bad Kandh, Damaru Kanta etc. Govind Singh, Sikru and Chandra Behera were captured on June 22, 1833. Govind was kept in confinement while Sikru *Zamindar*, Jagabandhu Babu, Rahu Biswal, Biju Dafadar, Damaru Pana, Narasingh Ghatua were hanged in August 1833.

Wilkinson realized that the queen was becoming more and more unpopular with passage of time. She had no hold over the tribal *Zamindar*s and people. She was weak in administration, but tyrannical in spirit. In fact, she was a puppet and danced to the tune of the British Government to save her throne. The Government realized that she should be removed as revolts, discontentment of the people against her rule became the order of the day. She was deposed from the throne in 1833.

Narayan Singh (1833-49)

Things did not improve, rather worsened when the British Government made the old, decrepit and imbecile Narayan Singh – an uncle of the Barapali *Zamindar* the ruler of Sambalpur on October 11, 1833. The *Gond* tribal chieftains were neither consulted nor invited to the ceremony of investiture. Taxes were increased. People were exploited in various ways. All those developments were paving the ground for untoward happenings.

Balaram Sai took opportunity of the situation of Sambalpur's political condition. He appealed to the tribal chieftains and people to help his nephew Surendra Sai obtain the throne. He liaisoned with Balabhadra Dao, Lakhanpur *Zamindar* who had already been against the queen Mohan Kumari and, thereafter, the king Naryan Singh. Surendra proceeded to Debrigarh fort on the Barapahar hill for discussions with Balabhadra Dao, the *Zamindar* of Lakhanpur. Narayan Singh learnt about it and sent forces to Debrigarh. The *Zamindar* was killed in the encounter, Surendra managed to escape. The killing of the *Zamindar* enraged the tribal people of his as well as other Zamindaris. Surendra exploited the situation in his favour. He came closer to the tribals, encouraging and inciting them against the British.

Surendra jumped to action. He attacked the Rajput *Zamindar* of Rampur. The *Zamindari* was taken away from a *Gond Zamindar* and given to Prananath Rajput for his help to Chhatra Sai (1691-1725) during his accession. The *Zamindar*'s house was set to fire and members of his family were killed. The incident was considered to be the revenge of the killing of Lakhanpur *Zamindar*. It made Surendra the idol and hero in the estimation of the tribals.

Imbued with a victory, Surendra proceeded towards Patna state en route Sambalpur. The Assistant Commissioner Maj. Ousley attacked Surendra's party at Budharaja Deheripali in the out skirt of Sambalpur town and arrested Surendra and his brother Udant, and uncle Balaram. They were given life-term imprisonment and sent to

Hazaribag jail in 1840. Balaram died in the jail.   Surendra and Udant were set free when the rebel Sepoys attacked the jail in 1857.

Developments 1840-57

Some significant changes took place in Sambalpur while Surendra Sai was in confinement at Hazaribag during 1840-57. Most important of them was the annexation of Sambalpur to the British Empire in 1849 by the Law of Escheat of Dalhousie following the death of Raja Narayan Singh without a heir to the throne. The three preceding decades (1817-49) of the British paramountcy had not set up a good track record of administration. The British Government remained completely apathetic to the weal and woe of the people during the rule of their stooges Rani Mohan Kumari (1827-33) and Narayan Singh (1833-49).   So the change from Chauhan monarchy to British Imperialism was in no way better.   The discontentment of the people and the *Zamindar*s went on growing.

The village headman (*gauntia*) and the *Zamindars* were kept in a state of terror. Rent-free villages and *muafis* they had been enjoying since generations were confiscated. The records reveal that while the annual revenue was 8,800 rupees before 1849, it increased to 74,000 in 1854[5].   It indicates the extortion made by the Government from the people. There were no leaders, no consciousness among the people who were mostly illiterate.   However, the ground was getting paved for untoward development in near future. In this connection, it may be pointed out that British Government made a fresh settlement of lands.

> The revenue was raised by one fourth indiscriminately,
> without reference to the capabilities of the villages and the

whole of the free-hold grants, religious and others were resumed. Those who held villages entirely rent free were assessed at half-rates, without any reference to the period for which the grants had been held or to the terms of the tenure. Assignments in money or grain from the revenue of villages were resumed as well as assignment of villages. Great dissatisfaction was consequently created at the outset and so seriously did the Brahmins who formed a numerous and powerful community, look upon it that they went in a body to Ranchi to appeal without, however, obtaining any redress. In 1854, by a second settlement of all villages, revenue was again raised by one-fourth. The result was an enormous rise in the revenue obtained by the Government[6].

It is said that king Narayan Singh alone has created 37 *muafis* in his reign. "The Raja's ministers and Brahmins possessed the best lands and obtained his sanction to all kinds of extortion; the former, in their turn, grind the ryots"[7]. It is well known that a Brahmin named Balakeshwar Dash of village Katapali near Bargarh, helped the king in the suppression of the *Gond* Rebellion of the early part of 19th century. He was killed by two *Gond* leaders Bandia Ray and Mahapatra Ray in 1843. They set fire to his house and took his eldest son Narayan Dash as a hostage to Debrigarh fort. His other son Krishna Dash and members of family sought refuse in Narayan Singh, the Raja of Sambalpur. The British Government instructed the king to grant Bargarh as *muafi* to them. It is known as *Sirkata* (grant for getting beheaded)[8].

However, to the authorities, the Principal Agent wrote that the tenure of the two *Garhotteas* of Bhukta and Ambabana were of recent origin. They had under their jurisdiction large tracts of country containing numerous villages held under *gounti* tenure. These produced complexity of rights often difficult to deal with. Hence, the two *Garhotteas* had to suffer under their new master[9].

The Principal Agent did not realize that the handling of the "land settlement in a country, accustomed to an age-old system of land tenure, would be like disturbing a hornet's nest and the opening up of a Pandora's box". The late Raja Narayan Singh had renewed the *pattas* four times, the first one for three years and, the latter ones for five years which had just expired[10]. It was immediately followed by a land settlement.

Not only the Brahmin *maufidars*, but also the tribal *Gauntias, Zamindars, Gartiahs, holders of Brahmottar and Devottar* lost their fiefs or could retain by payment of rent. It raised a great hue and cry throughout the length and breadth of the tract among both tribal and non-tribal segments of fief-holders.

However, the authorities kept their eyes and ears shut since their own positions were precarious. The situation was described as:

> "The British had been very keen in sending remittances to the British exchequer. The more the merrier, because the remittances determined the recognition of their services. The appreciation usually came in the form of a citation or the award of a knighthood. After amassing plenty of wealth during their sojourn in India these decorations, gave them the status to present themselves in rich and fashionable society on their return to England. These British officers were so very crazy to receive a decoration from the Crown that no action appeared to be immoral. The *garhotteas* of Bhukta and Ambabona were deposed because "they were found to be guilty of oppression and extortion by the Principal Agent"[11].

The Brahmins became resentful of the terms of the Settlement. They met Cadenhead, the first Principal Assistant Commissoner of Sambalpur and pointed out the violation of Paragraph 6 of the Proclamation of Queen Victoria which read:

> But it is the intention of the Hon'ble Company's Government that arrangements may be made to maintain the rights and privileges of individuals of all sorts in the same manner as they were established in the time of the deceased Raja and theretofore.

The Brahmins sought a second interview with Cadenhead and when the latter threatened them they left for Chota Nagpur to meet the Agent[12]. The Agent Mr. Crawford did not agree with the Brahmins' contention of the contravention of the Paragrah's provision in the Proclamation. He rather argued:

> …….. that they (the Brahmins) had no rights and privileges whatsoever, for the Brahmins themselves will scarcely deny that of which the records of this office furnish abundant proof that Narayan Singh (the king) resumed and assessed many tenures comprising some granted by himself as well as others granted by his predecessors and consequently the tenures which we found in existence had endured only through his sufferance not by virtue of any rights or privileges possessed by the occupants[13].

Crawford in very clear terms told the Brahmins that they would be required to pay rent as a guarantee of their continued enjoyment. The result of non-payment was resumption as the other alternative[14]. In fact, many of the *Muafis, Brahmottar* and *Devottar* grants were very old. As pointed out, such grants are made in perpetuity, with all appurtenances like wood, stone, tree, fish, shadow and boundaries of them as long as the sun and the moon endure. The usurper is warned that if one takes away land granted by himself or others, he ruts for six thousand years as worms in the hell (vide Narayan Singh's Sirkkata grant of Bargarh referred to above). How could he resume the grant? If he had done so, as pointed by A. Das[15] he must have done so at the instance of the British Government.

It is observed:

> The rebellion was mainly centered round the strongholds of the *Gonds* and Binjhal *Zamindars* who had a feeling that their powers would be usurped by the British Government. It may be stated that Sambalpur and the adjoining territories were mainly inhabited by aboriginal tribes. Xxxxxxxxx They had a genuine apprehension that for their support to Surendra Sai, they have to part with their best lands to be assigned as *jagir, debottar* or *brahmottar*[16].

The dispossession of the Brahman *maufidars* of 62 villages, *Brahmottar* of 37 villages and, importantly, the *garhotteas* of Ambabhana and Bhukta of late shown the way the wind was blowing. The threats and misdemeanour made to the Rajas of Bamra, Rairakhol, Shakti and Sarangarh etc. made them indignant against the British Government. The curtailment of the powers of the *Gauntias* with regards to trial of civil cases, the impositions of various kinds of fees, penalties, cesses and, importantly, stamp duty created dissatisfaction among people at large.

Apart from the Brahmins, the tribal people who were farmers and soldiers under *Zamindars* were shaken by the new settlement and policy of the Government. The people had learnt the evil effects of the British Settlement made in the neighbouring Singhbum. At the height of things, came the resumption of the land granted to the goddess, Samaleswari venerated by tribal and non-tribal alike. Thus, all the people were brought or coming closer by circumstances created by the British rule. It may be pointed out that both the Brahmins and castes of non-tribal stock as well as tribals had worked hand in hand against the British during the Mutiny years. Many of the Brahmin

Gauntias had suffered from fine, imprisonment and execution for their role in the support of the Rebellion 1857.

Gondmaru

Even after suppression the revolts of Bheden and, then of Surendra Sai and sending him to Hazaribag jail, king Narayan Singh could not restore peace and order in the kingdom. The *Gond* tribal people indulged in looting, arson and murder in broad day light. The actions of the king could not cope with the situation. It was a sort of chaos in anarchy. The *Zamindar* of Pahadsirgida[17] took leadership of the sort of activities which became popular as *Gondmaru* (literally killing by *Gonds*). The Raja employed Balunkeswar Dash of Katapali to deal with the *Gonds* but he was killed. This has been described earlier in connection with *Sirkata* grant of 1843.

References

1. *Bengal District Gazetteers, Sambalpur*, Calcutta, 1909 (hereinafter referred to as *O'Malley's*) p. 27.

2. *Sambalpur, 1971*, p. 357.

3. *ibid,* p. 360.

4. Kumar Hasan : *Sambalpurara Swadhinata Sangrama* (Oriya), Sambalpur University, 2001 (hereinafter referred to as *Sangrama, 2001*), pp. 83 ff.

5. Sahu, J.K. : *Odisha Itihāsa*, II, Cuttack, (not dated), p.   (hereinafter referred to as *OI*).

6. *O'Malley's*

7. M. Kittoe : *Journey through the Forests of Orissa, JASB*, May, 1839.

8. The text of the grant written in Oriya as quoted in *Itihasa, 1968*, p. 337.

9. Letter No. 11 dated 21 Sep. 1850 from Principal Agent, Sambalpur to Commissioner, Chota Nagpur.

10. Letter No. 40 day, 1835 from Principal Agent, Sambalpur to Commissioner, Chhot Nagpur (Orissa State Archives : Sambalpur Papers), Bhubaneswar.

11. *Surendra Sai, 2001*, p. 84.

12. Letter No. 104 dated 11 Nov. 1856 from Cadenhead to Crawford; Letter No. 86 dated 3.10.50 (O.C.O. No. 3 of Board of Revenue, Cuttack's Record Room).

13. Letter from Crawford to Cadenhead No. 70, 19 Oct. 1850.

14. *ibid.*

15. *Life*, p. 50.

16. *ibid,* p. 38.

17. Sahu, N.K. : *Veer Surendra Sai*, Bhubaneswar, 1989 (hereinafter referred to as *Veer Surendra, 1985*), pp. 62-63.

CHAPTER 3

EARLY PHASE OF THE REVOLUTION

Sambalpur Tract of Orissa had been associated with the 1857 Mutiny right from

its early phase in 31 July 857 when the mutinous sepoys of the Ramgarh Battalion attacked and broke open the gates of Hazaribag jail, in which the two brothers Surendra Sai of Khinda *Zamindari* and his brother Udant Sai were set free. They had been kept in the jail, as pointed out in the previous Chapter, at the instance of the Sambalpur king by the British authorities, since 1840 because Surendra staked claim to the throne of Sambalpur. In the mean time, Sambalpur kingdom was escheated to the British Indian Empire in 1849. The two brothers started their journey towards Sambalpur. The British Government was afraid that he might raise a standard of revolt for restoration of Sambalpur Raj for himself and became perturbed. The release and journey of Surendra Sai to Sambalpur might appear to be a trivial event, but the policy of the British Government to annex Sambalpur kingdom to the British Indian Empire and unpopularity of the administration on the one hand and popular support to the cause of Surendra Sai on the other, even when he was in confinement at Hazaribag, came as a headache to the Sambalpur administration. As apprehended, popular support came pouring in when it was heard that Surendra had been on his way to Sambalpur.

Although the kingdom had been abolished and an unpopular king, a puppet of the British Government, had gone, yet the *Zamindars* who counted about sixteen, of the erstwhile *Raj* could not reconcile themselves with new British *Raj*. The majority of them were still after restoration of the *Raj*, with the most legitimate claimant Surendra Sai as the king. The British Government, on their part was more intent on preserving their rule, by any means – fair or foul, and collecting more money rather than pacifying the discontented feudal lords and their people whose customary rights and privileges, as discussed in the previous Chapter, had been taken away and popular sentiment had been hurt during the last eight years of their occupation. Never did the British Government realize that the *Zamindars* were a prop of to the kings and a source of inspiration and leadership to the illiterate but brave, fighting-like and loyal tribal people of a hinterland of the country. Thus, the trivial event of the release of Surendra Sai marked the beginning of a revolution which continued for full five years, 1857 to 1862, with far-reaching effects.

Unique Features

The release of the two brothers has been considered as heralding a new phase of "Revolution of 1857". It was, in fact, a continuum of

> The earlier revolutions in Sambalpur directed against the British started in 1827 and continued up to 1840 when the great hero Surendra Sai was overpowered and taken as captive. The revolution of 1857 in Sambalpur may be taken to be a further continuation of the revolution of 1827 with a respite of 17 years which Surendra Sai spent behind the prison bars at Hazaribagh. In fact, the Sambalpur revolution which started in 1827 and continued up to 1862, four years after the revolution in India was stamped out, is considered to be one and the whole as the same leader conducted the entire movement with the same purpose of driving the British out of Sambalpur region[1].

In his letter dated 9 August 1857 the Commissioner of Chhotanagpur has informed the Principal Assistant Agent of Sambalpur that two Companies of the 8th Ramgarh Battalion had freed Surendra and Udant from the prison and were escorting 'the two pretenders' to Sambalpur "with a view to establishing a *Rajah*". It indicates that the escorting Sepoys had sympathy with the cause of Surendra to become the king of Sambalpur. R.K. Mishra has observed:

> The mutineers, who were active all over North India, wanted to gain the maximum mileage against the Imperial Power, wherever they noticed a weak-link. They realised the strategic importance of Sambalpur in gaining access to the rest of the region in Eastern India[2].

Another unique feature was that in all other cases the individual claimants who were deprived of their thrones fought alone with their army or received the assistance of the mutinied Sepys – in some others. In the case of Sambalpur, all the rulers of the erstwhile confederated States under Sambalpur unitedly appealed for the restoration of the Sambalpur Raj. It shows the loving affection of the people for continuance of Chauhana dynasty in Sambalpur. Since the most legitimate claimant Surendra was available, they pleaded for the restoration of the kingdom under his kingship. It shows the loyal patriotism of the people for the mother land.

Again, it has rightly been pointed out:

> The participants (of the Rebellion) took recourse mostly to non-violent methods similar to the struggle launched later under the leadership of Mahatma Gandhi. These methods were submission of petitions, sending deputations and observing peaceful non-cooperation like "no-tax-campaign".....[3]

Unlike other regions of the country where all sections of people did not take part in the fighting of the local *Rajahs* and *Zamindars* against the British Government, almost all the sections of people cutting across lines of caste and status wholeheartedly participated in the Rebellion. A number of Brahmin *Gauntias* as well as people came out secretly to organize people. For example, Padmanabh Guru, Loknath Panda, Mrityunjay Panigrahi, Ganesh Upadhyaya etc. were some of the distinguished Brahmin headmen. The people did not consider that Surendra was fighting to get Sambalpur throne or the *Zamindars* to obtain their rights and privileges. In fact, the people in general were against the British Government.

The sentiment of the people at large was hit hard when land and villages granted for maintaining the worship of the premier goddess of the Tract Samaleswari were taken away by the Government. Fuel was added to fire when the tribal soldiers in the king's army and feudal lords' retinues lost their services and land they enjoyed thereof.

Samaleswari temple, as noted by Impey[4], had attained a special status in the socio-religious life of the people not only of Sambalpur but the eighteen *Garhjats* which were under Sambalpura's suzerainty.   The contributions to the goddess which were withdrawn during Land Settlements created disaffection among the people. Further, the resumption of *Brahmottar* and *Dharmottar* lands to Brahmins, as observed by H.B. Impey, was at the root of all discontent. He tried to appease the feelings of such land grantees, when he came as Deputy Commissioner of Sambalpur in 1861. He has observed:

> Not only the Government displayed conscious neglect of the vital interests of the natives in matters most fundamental to their day to day living, they also attempted to manifest an utter disregard for the powers and prestige of the privileged classes as a result of which, they had developed contempt for these British officers[4a].

It may be pointed out that such grants, which were enjoyed rent-free for services by the grantees, were charged at fifty percent of the normal rates in 1850 – which not only enraged the Brahmins but also 'added to the revolutionary zeal of the fighting community'.

Again, unlike other regions of the country, the Sambalpur Rebellion was provided leadership by majority of the *Zamindars, Garhtteas* and *Gauntias.* They were staunch supporters of Surendra Sai and inveterate enemies of the British. Of course, they took directions from Surendra as and when they were in need of them. In those days, it was difficult to contact, co-ordinate and plan operations in various theatres situated amidst jungles, hills and valleys under one man, it goes to the credit of Surendra and some *Zamindars* and members of their families to organize and implement their actions[4b] – particularly when the British authorities were alert about encountering any action on the part of rebels.

The only cause which inspired the people was driving out the British Raj and restoring Chauhana kingdom at Sambalpur. Although illiterate, the people at large were loyal to their respective feudal lords – *Zamindars* or *Garhtteas* or *Gauntias* most of whom were dedicated to Suredra Sai. Surendra's name was a magic, his charisma whether he was seen or not worked wonders in the Tract. Even where a king or a *Zamindar* was against the Rebellion, the people of his State or estate supported the cause of Surendra. Even where the king or a *Zamindar* was afraid to help the rebels publicly, as in the case of Khariar's king Krishna Chandra Singh Deo, he lent a helping hand secretly. The *Zamindars, Garhtteas* and *Gauntias* and the like of not only Sambalpur but of the Feudatory states surrounding Sambalpur were active sympathizers and sometimes rendered help for which some of them like the kings of Patna, Bamra and Khariar were warned/fined sometimes. Thus, though a comparatively unknown figure that Surendra was till very late or a hinterland that the

Tract was, the rebellion in the Tract which has been sidelined thus far, deserves a befitting place in the annals of 1857 Mutiny.

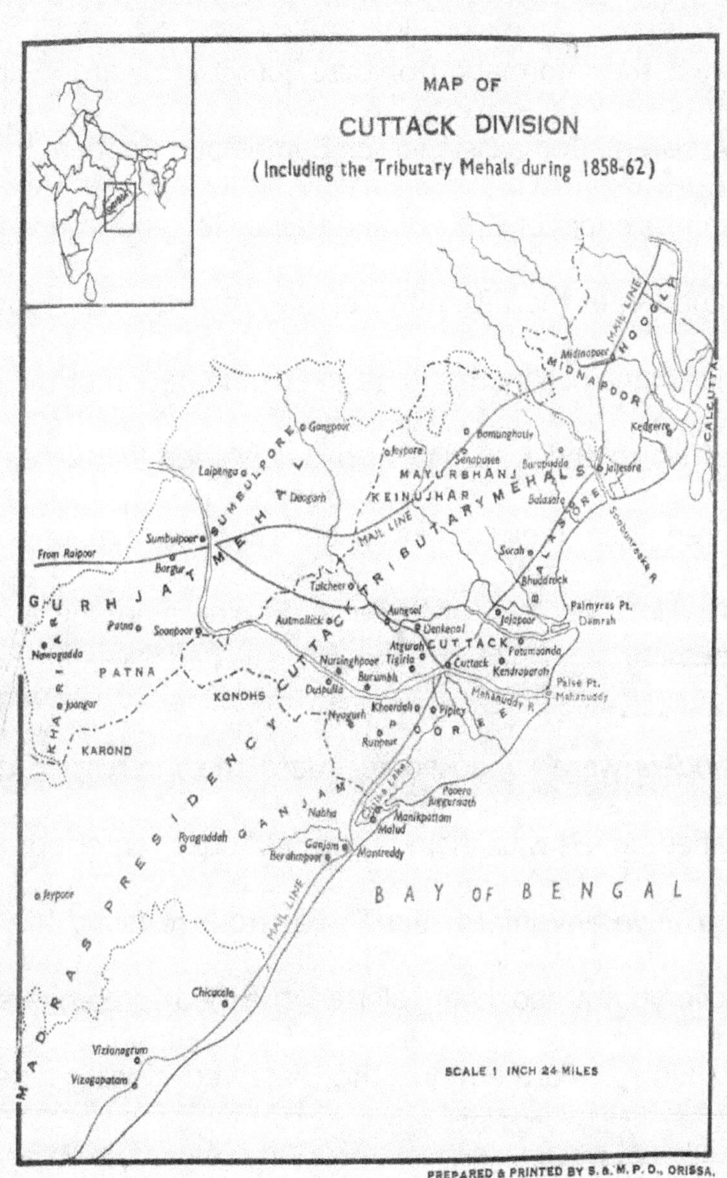

PREPARED & PRINTED BY S. & M. P. O., ORISSA.

Surendra's March from Hazaribag to Sambalpur

The march of Surendra and his brother Udant from Hazaribag to Sambalpur, accompanied by 1,000 to 1200 armed men of 8th Ramgarh Battalion[5], was a historic one. After receiving the information of their journey towards Sambalpur on 9 August 1857 Principal Assistant Commissioner of Sambalpur Captain R.T. Leigh sent urgent messages to Commissioners of Cuttack and Raipur to send troops to Sambalpur to meet any untoward situation in the aftermath of their arrival. The Governor of Bengal was also worried about that since by that time the conflagration of the *sepoys* had spread to different parts of North India. Leigh also despatched *parwanas* to all the *Rajas* and *Zamindars* to strengthen their defences and apprise him of information about the advancing party[6]. However, except three land holders no one evinced interest as Cap. Leign has noted[7].

The *Zamindars* were supposed to guard the interest of their Imperial Master, according to treaties signed with them but to his "utter regret not a single *Gauntia* nor a *Zamindar* cared to give any information". Far from resisting the advance of Surendra Sai, for which everybody had been alerted the two 'pretenders' had an unopposed progress in the country. Furthermore, they received rousing reception from people of all castes and sections.

> The absence of Surendra and Udant for seventeen long years from Sambalpur had enhanced their admiration and love for these two leaders, who were held so dear to their heart. Many looked upon them as demigods and drew analogy of the advent of the two leaders in Sambalpur with the mythological heroes, lord Krishna and his brother Balaram's visit to Mathura, on the invitation of Kansa the demon king[8].

Cap. Leigh became perturbed when he did not find people's inclination for the British Government. On the other hand, people came by their hundreds to greet Surendra on the way. Leigh reported to Cuttack Commissioner Cockburn that "the people of Sambalpur do not exhibit any strong feeling towards the Government"[9]. He urged the Commissioners of Cuttack and Raipur to send troops as early as possible. In a letter to Cap. Dalton, Cap. Leigh wrote:

> It is a very anxious time for us in this isolated spot and no
> help seems to be likely to arrive for a long time to come[10].

The nervousness of Cap. Leigh may be known from the fact that he was keeping a boat ready to transfer Mrs. Leigh and some others to a safe place in case of any untoward situation[11].

Cap. Leigh took all sorts of precautionary measures to cope with the situation that might arise following arrival of Surendra and his party in Sambalpur. The Cuttack Commissioner was observing the situation with concern when he could not send forces due to heavy rains and flood in the Mahanadi. The troops might face encounters and tribulations and might fall short of supplies while passing through marshy lands and rivers without bridges in the Tributary States. Cap. Leigh, finding delay in the arrival of forces and apprehending the arrival of Surendra and his party at Sambalpur any time, went to the extent of declaring a reward of Rs. 250 for capture of the "two pretenders".

A dilemma came to prevail in Commissioner's Office at Cuttack regarding despatch of troops. Whereas Major Bates, the Officer Commanding had made ready a contingent of troops to send to Sambalpur, Commissioner Cockburn was hesitant. The latter was afraid of the fact that if Surendra was accompanied by one or two Companies of soldiers, the forces of 40th Madras Native Infantry(hereinafter referred to as MNI) that would be sent from Cuttack, might join them or the former might rise in revolt suspecting the latter for coming to disarm them. Finally, probably under pressing demands of Cap. Leigh, two Companies of 40th MNI were despatched, with ten elephants to ferry supplies across the rivers, under command of Cap. Hawkins accompanied by Lt. Hart and Ensign Napier. However, Cockburn was in constant touch with the Sambalpur administration for information till the arrival of the troops at Sambalpur[12].

With passage of every day, fresh problems were arising and the feeling of insecurity of Cap. Leigh was increasing. A number of sepoys were getting sick. Leigh dared not send troops to check the progress of the march of   Surendra's party for he was afraid they might join the soldiers escorting Surendra Sai. Communication through *Dak* with Cuttack, and more so with Calcutta and Bombay was becoming difficult and insecure. He again requested the Commissioner of Cuttak to send three more Companies of the 40th Regiment of MNIto cope with the situation that might arise in the aftermath of Surendra's arrival at Sambalpur[12a].

The itinerary of Surendra and party was not known. One researcher[12b] is of the view that they accompanied the mutinous soldiers, who made them free, went to Chainbasa to join the rebellion in Singhbhum. They found there that the Mutiny was in an 'indefinite shape' and so decided to proceed to Sambalpur. Whatever be the case, the same scholar has written that Surendra and party "traveled through forest track 'almost unaided' facing great hazards as the rainfall was heavy and they had to cross many flooded hill streams". They fell seriously ill on the way which delayed their march to Sambalpur. They passed through the Feudatory State of Gangpur and by the time their whereabouts was known to the British administrators, they were found camping with large number of followers in the jungles near Sason village about six miles off Sambalpur town early in October 1857.

Surendra's Arrival at Sambalpur : Political Developments

Surendra Sai with 1000 or 1200 armed men entered Sambalpur in the morning of 7th October 1857. They came in a huge procession to Sambalpur Garh. A large number of people, including some Zamindars and their relations, about 15,000 attended the meeting. Two resolutions were adopted –

(i)   remission of the remainder of life imprisonment of Surendra and Udant

(ii)   to see a *Rajah* established in Sambalpur.

The people decided to move peacefully and submit petitions and sending delegations to authorities to achieve their purposes. They decided to adopt 'non-cooperation' and 'no-tax campaign' to pressurize the government concede to the demands[13].

As to the Government, Cap. Leigh did not want to take up arms against the Surendra and his party. He wanted to know the real intentions. Secondly, the troops in Sambalpur were not sufficient to indulge in encounters. Further, the Ramgarh troops at Sambalpur had 'wavering tendency'. The people were to a large extent in support of the 'pretender' to the throne of Sambalpur. He wrote to both the Commissioners of Chhotanagpur and Cuttack apprising them of the situat6ion at Sambalpur[13b]. The

Commissioner of Cuttack also apprehended 'large scale defection in his armed forces to be deployed at Sambalpur'. Leigh sent two *parwanas* to Surendra to appear before him without delay[14]. Surendra met Leigh on the guarantee of safety of his life. Two petitions – one for his and another for Udant's remission of the sentence of imprisonment were submitted. The following day, 8th October 1857 Surendra met Cap. Leigh for the second time. Leigh asked him to disband his forces and lie in wait for the orders of the Government on their petitions.

Leigh informed Surendra, through one Chhakadi Mahapatra who was sent as an envoy, to surrender first before his case might be taken up by Government. Leigh played treachery and arrested Surendra. However, Surendra managed to escape from the confinement with the help of the sentries and Chhakadi Mahapatra. He ran away to Khinda where Udant had gone earlier to organize support for the rebellion. Thus, Leigth's plan to keep him in confinement failed.

In the mean time, the two petitions from Surendra and Udanta, recommended by Leigh to the Commissioner of Cuttack were rejected. The Government was against the proposal of restoring Sambalpur kingdom. Rather the Government wanted Surendra to reside at Cuttack as a proof of unconditional surrender. However, Leigh and the Commissioner of Cuttack were afraid of the consequences of such action. It is evident from the letter of the Commissioner to Governor of Bengal dated 30 October 1857:

> Private information lead me to believe that strong sympathies for Sruendra Sai and Ouddant Sai is felt, and evinced by the people of Sambalpur, and all their followers have dispersed for the time being, the heads of many

> villages are still collected and ready to reassemble their adherents when it is supposed proper to do so, much depending upon the reply of the Government to the petition for pardon, by the two leaders[15].

He further submitted that

> It is absolutely necessary that early and decisive measures of some kind be taken at Sambalpur for I am greatly apprehensive that the spirit of disaffection was not only spreading out, that the rebels and mutineers, driven away from elsewhere, may take services in these wild and distant tracts if by doing so, they can embarrass the Government, while all the inhabitants being once committed to a course contrary to what is right, may not easily be reclaimed[16].

The deployment of a large number of troops and secret correspondences in the Government circles could not go unnoticed by the supporters of Surendra Sai. Sambalpur in those days was a small township confined to an area between present Kunjel Para up to Kutchery and, without a permanent jail or spacious bungalow for high officials including Principal Assistant Commissioner. The arrival of two Companies of Madras Native Infantry on 5 September 1857, followed by six Companies infantry and a few detachments of Artillery squad of Ramgarh Battalion created panic among the general people. Many people were reported to have left the township, tribals had left for their 'natural habitat' in the hills and jungles mzny others were ready in the event of any untoward situation. A section of sepoys had sympathy with the people and the rebels and, were against any drastic step against the rebels. They were ready to change to the side of the rebels, if such a situation would occur. Cap. Leigh expected that after arrival of three Companies of 40th Regiment of MNI, the activities of the unruly mob could be suppressed[17].

The Spies of the Government reported the gathering of large crowds in several villages. A gathering of 1000/1200 men at Khinda was reported by two men of 40th M.N.I. and also of 60 armed men proceeding towards Kolabira from Khinda. The *Gartia* of Kolabira, a strong supporter of rebels, was reported to have assembled 200 armed men and, in the case of necessity, could muster 8,000 men to fight against the Government troops. Many such pieces of news circulated amidst Government circles.

As to the principal rebel Surendra, he remained calm and quiet, awaiting the decision on his petitions, in confinement. He got scent of the evil intentions of the Government. He learnt the concentrations of troops at Sambalpur and realised his insecurity. With the help of some sentris and Chhakdi Mahapatra who came as an envoy of Leigh for parleys with Surendra, he escaped from the confinement in the night of 31 October 1857. He proceeded straight to Khinda where his brother Udant was waiting for him with an armed group of 1000 men. The Commissioner of Cuttack felt that Surendra has "duped the authorities by posing his peaceful intention. He was, indeed, playing a double game"[18]. He further remarked that "it is unfortunate that they were not seized and executed, as soon as they came to know of their followers had not actually dispersed"[19]. He assured Leigh all sorts of help to stamp out any rebellion and eliminate the rebel-leaders.

The people of Sambalpur were equally disappointed. Their main concern was restoration of Sambalpur *Raj*, which they hoped would be fulfilled through peaceful settlement. The matter also touched the king of Bamra who sent a petition to the Assistant superintendent of Tributary Mahals, Cuttack in support of the cause of

Surendra Sai[20]. The king was threatened with the dire consequences of imprisonment of life and confiscation of his estate like that of the Angul king[21].

"The escape of Surendra Sai heralded the beginning of the revolution of Sambalpur against the British and people from all parts of the distinct flocked in large number under his banner to fight for the liberation of Sambalpur from the alien yoke".

The show of appeasement on the part of the British Government on one side and peace on the part of the rebels or people on the other for a couple of months was 'only to buy time' for both the parties to make themselves ready for the untoward developments. If the Government was in need of more troops and arms and time to study the prevailing condition, the rebels were in need of time to gain more adherents, arms and organize public support for their cause.

Preparation for Confrontation

It was only a matter of time for both the Government and the rebels to confront each other. The leaders of the people *Gauntias, Gartias, Zamindars* returned disappointed to their villages and estates after nothing was done by the Government to restore Sambalpur kingdom. They became enraged to learn about the arrest of Surendra and started to organize for an impending confrontation with the British Government. Their authority in their respective estates was unquestionable. They were also popular. Many of them had been maintaining armed retainers since the *Raj* was there and, had not disbanded them with abolition of the *Raj.* It was reported that the later Sambalpur Rajas have introduced guns and muskets. They have fought successfully against the Marathas four/five decades ago. Importantly they knew utilizing the jungle and hilly terrain and the mode of warfare befitting to it. The guerrilla warfare was well known to them.

That the people of the whole of Sambalpur Tract had participated at different times and operations, as known from a despatch, dated 9 February 1858, of Deputy Commissioner of Sambalpur to Cap. Dalton, the officiating Commissioner of Chhatisgarh[22]. Except a few, it included the names of all important *Zamindars, Garohtteas* and *Gountias*. They were as follows:

1.   Surendra Sai   - Mutineer from Hazaribag

2.   Ouddant Sai   -   -do-

3.   Dhoorup Sai   - Scion of Chauhans

4.   Ojjal Sai   -   -do-

5.   Medini Sai   -   -do-

6.   Chhabila Sai   -   -do-

7.   Jugal Sai   -   -do-

8.   Mitrabhanu Sai   - S/o Surendra Sai

9.   Karina Naik   - S/o Banamali Naik

10.   Khuggo Naik   - S/o Banamali Naik, Zamindar of Kolabira

11.   Deria Singh   - S/o Narahari, Garohttea of Rampur

12.   Dhun Singh   - Zamindar of Deori

13.   J. Hatte Singh   - Garhottea of Ghess

14.   Arjun   - Garohttea of Luisingh

15.   Chandra   - S/o Arjun, Garohttea of Luisingh

16. Manohar singh   - Zamindar of Bhedan

17. Markanda Bereha   - Badasambar *Zamidnar* (Borasambar)

18. Dhyal Bohidar   - *Zamindar* of Bheden

19. Danardan Singh   - *Zamindar* of Pahadsirgida

20. Arkhito Gountia   - *Gountia* of Mundamohal

21. Kripasindhu Beriha   - Bamara

22. Sadasiv Majhi   - Gangpur

23. Kamal Singh   - S/o Dhun Singh, *Zamindari of* Deoree

24. Pitambar Singh   - Zamindar of Korunda

25. Mahadev Gountia   - Rampore

26. Dhun Singh   - Louisingha.

Operations Begin : Problems

The Government geared its forces to stamp out the Rising by capturing Surendra Sai and his brother Uddant Sai. Leigh informed Dalton that "he had received report that there were a thousand or twelve hundred men assembled at Khinda and subsequently proceeded towards Kolabira. Immediately following the escape of Surendra Sai from the old fort, where he was kept under the British custody, Leigh the Principal Assistant Commissioner held a conference of his officers. Since Surendra Sai was most likely to have taken shelter in his home at Khinda or anywhere around his village, they decided to pursue military operations in that direction.. Apprehending stiff resistance from the enemy with the support of a large number of armed supporters, the British troops marched on the morning of 4 November 1857 towards Khinda. The British authorities were aware that the followers who had joined in the forces of Surendra Sai were mostly civilians and hence, instead of taking resort to military actions, they had planned to disperse them.

The first operation of the British troops began with a strength of two companys of 40 MNI, thirty men of the Ramgad Battalion, six divisions of Sawars, thirty *sibundies* two Howtizers with a detachment of *Golundaz*. Captain Knocker was the Commander of the forces, assisted by Lt. Hadow. and Rup Singh Bahadur, the former Dewan of Narain Singh. The latter was instructed to provide intelligence information about the enemy hide-outs. The operation was kept a close secret. After conducting the operation, which ended in a fiasco, Knockker reported Leigh with a detailed account of

67

Battle of Jharghaty, 5 November 1857

> "I went with a detachment of the above strength, I left for Jharghatty at which Ghats the Rebels were believed to have collected". These were usually narrow passes between two hills ranges. Usually, the route in the hill-terrain passes through these *ghats*. In the alternative one has to climb the entire hill to reach the other side which would be time consuming, and a tiring process. These narrow gorges provided suitable ground for taking a defensive position, to intercept and harass the enemy. The hill ranges in Sambalpur were full of such narrow defiles because of the existence of several hill ranges located in compact areas. These areas cover several hundreds of square miles. Unless one is escorted by a well conversant guide, he was sure to miss the way and very likely would be a convenient catch in an ambush laid by the enemy.

Knockker while describing the campaign adds "Having reached that village about nine miles from Sambalpur town learning that no news of our coming has preceded, we marched with utmost despatch with the object of being there, before they could get any information".   In the march through dense forests, they could not see anybody except groups of three or four persons at three or four places. Those persons whom they had come across, might have been ordinary villagers going to their usual errands but to the army of Knockker, everyone moving about appeared to be a supporter of Surendra Sai. Whether the rebels had really mustered there, anticipating the march of the Britishers in that direction, or had gathered there, preparing for an attack, is difficult to say. But the fact remains, that as Knockker reported to Leigh "the rebels were completely concealed from us in the dense jungles covering the hills to our right, left and front, but they maintained continuous fire, for about 20 minutes by which we had one man wounded mortally and another lightly". Instead of a reconnaissance, Knockker straightway ordered for firing in the air a few rounds of Cannister shells while two of his parties were climbing the hills in the direction wherefrom the sounds of muskets were coming. By firing, the Britishers had already made their position and the weapons they were equipped with revealed to the rebels. Hence, the Rebels took to safer positions which could not be located by the two parties sent for combing the hills in search of the enemy. The two detachments of troops returned without finding any rebel. He however wrote in his report

> "One party came upon what was evidently a supply depot, containing rice and Atta and gram to the amount of 18 elephant loads, this being unable to carry it away, was destroyed as far as possible. We halted for three hours on the foot of the hills and then proceeded towards Kolabira".

The ration items, it is difficult to say whether belonged to the rebels or the villagers of the surrounding area, who fearing the loot and pillage of their property, experienced under the Marathas might have taken those to maintain them till the return of the British troops.

Campaign against Kolabira

However, not being able to trace any enemy, the forces commanded by Knockker marched in the direction of Kolabira. At Kolabira which was deserted" they halted in front of the house of the *Garahottea*. Kolabira was a big village. Its *Zamindar* Karunakar was a leading activist (of the rebellion).It was stated that the *Zamindar* had collected two hundred men ready to fight and a strength of 8000 that could easily be mustered at a short notice. Hence the village of Kolabira was completely deserted , but there was no one to corroborate the fact that the news of the campaign by the British had been known earlier and the villagers had left the village with their rations which would be required for the period of their short stay during their sojourn in an outside place.

Knockker, while halting in front of the house of the *Garhottea* discovered "loophole in walls for fire arms and gate closed". He learnt that those were meant to be used to fire muskets at the enemy from behind walls of the house of the *Zamindar*. He suspected presence of armed retainers inside, he sent a contingent of force (Howitzers) into the house. "I directed Lt. Hadow to fire at the house and we marched to our halting place", Knockker had written. It is observed:

> The operation of Kolabira so far as the report of Knockker is concerned reads like one of the nature of a flag March, aimed to inject a sense of fear and terrorize the enemy with a view to effect the dispersals of any combination. They were definitely successful in making a demonstration of the strength of the fire arm and the strength of their troops, which could be deployed against the rebels.

March to Khinda

The report continued to state: "On the 8th instant, visited Khinda and finding in Surendra Sai and Ouddant Sai's houses, similar preparations had been made for fighting we followed the same course", that is, sending a detachment of warriors inside their house and firing a few rounds of cannons on their houses. Knockker concluded his report by writing "we returned this day and I have every reason to believe that the rebels are totally dispersed"[24]. In connection with Kolabira and Khinda it is remarked:

It was the first major expedition and hence it was bound to have a significant repercussion on the players and the participants in this war game[24a].

Reaction of People

The dissatisfaction amongst the people began to grow more on account of the operations of the British army at Jharghti, Kolabira and Khinda. It has rightly been observed:

> One very significant development following the display of the British strength through these army movements was the harassment experienced b the innocent civilians. If at all there was any movement, it could be only a mass demonstration of the displeasure of the people towards the British rule and their actions. The other purpose was to indicate their solidarity behind the native rule under Surendra Sai[25].

The people rose to the occasion. They tried to cut off all communications by raising barricades along the roads and thereby blockaded the passage of the British troops. The "insurgency" revolution meanwhile, spread into the distant regions like Kondhmal, borders of Raipur and to almost all parts of Sambalpur. The general technique adopted by them was mostly peaceful. Their purpose was to cut off all communications. In the Road connecting Bombay and Calcutta, two Dak Chowkees were burnt and some wallets were destroyed. Same thing happened at Jujumura also. On the Sambalpur-Ranchi Road, communications were also cut-off and Daks intercepted. Local leaders the *Gountias* and *Garhotteas* took part in organizing the disaffection amongst the people.

Strategy of the Rebels

The military operations of Kolabira and Khinda of the British army made the rebels change their strategy as well as area of operation. They realised that even in the hills and jungles they should not fight face to face with the enemy, but in a hide-and-seek manner, what is called guerrilla warfare in groups, for which the terrain was quite useful. Surprise attacks would be more dangerous to the enemy. Appearing at one place and suddenly disappearing from there, attacks through traditional weapons of javelin, bow and arrow, axe and sword and even boulders, barricading the passage of enemy were thought to be ideal for the landscape. That would harass the enemies whose troops trained in the warfare of plains could not cope with the modi operandi of the rebels.

Secondly, since the Sambalpur rebellion found support in not only distant *Zamindaris* such as Ghess, Borasambar of the Tract but also in the surrounding Native States of Patna, Khariar and Bamra to some extent and also in such distant *Zamindaris* as Phuljhar, Deori, Sonakhan of present Chhatisgarh – the rebellion should be made more widespread by taking such places under operation. In that case, the British forces would be divided and they would find it very difficult to face the many-pronged disturbances arising from different quarters.

For the objectives in view, the rebels planned to isolate the British forces, i.e. keep them confined in Sambalpur as far as possible, by cutting off the lines of communication. For that purpose they planned setting up five strategic points at passage of hills – two on the road of Sambalpur-Nagpur, two on Sambalpur-Ranchi and one on Sambalpur-Cuttack. Singhora near Sohela which had already served as an outpost to check Mararthas incursions from Nagpur, was placed in the supervision of the valiant *Zamindar* of Ghens Madho Singh and his sons of Kunjel, Hatte (Hathi) and

Bairi. The other was Pahadsirgida which was looked after by *Zamindar* Janardan Singh. Similarly, the Jharghaty and Maula-Bhanja passes on the Ranchi road were in the care of Udant Sai, Surendra's brother. The Badpati (also known as Gadghati) in Munder-Luisingh hill range on the Cuttack road was guarded by Chadra Garhottea of Luisingh. The most important stronghold was Debrigarh in the Barpahar hill range was guarded by Kamal Singh and Khageswar Singh, son and grandson respectively of Balabhadra Deo, the late *Zamindar* of Lakhanpur who was killed in an encounter by Sambalpur king's army in 1837. All the five passes were fortified by construction of thick and lofty walls made of boulders and mud. Besides the garrison inside such fortresses led by eminent Zamindars and their scions and advance guards were deployed at different places surrounding them.

The general idea of a fortification may be gathered from a letter of Ensign Warlow, to Lt. Governor of Bengal[26]. He has enclosed a sketch map of the area of the Pahardsirgida Pass which he invaded in February 1858. His report says that a wall of boulders thirty feet long and seven feet high was erected at the base of the pass between two high hills, whiled another wall was constructed almost midway between the base and the top to the left and the third was made at the top. The lower barricades may be seen from the topmost. Besides all the trees on the paths leading to the walls were cleaned so that the movement of the enemy troops might be known and arrows might be shot. Importantly, it is said, Surendra or his top-aides stationed in the centrally situated Debrigarh could move among the passes in the same night. That sort of vigilance and co-ordination – the need of the hour – 'baffled the military skill and strategy of the British officers for a long time'.

Jujomora Incident

The rebels kept themselves ready for encounters at different places. The first principal event came to happen at Jujomora between Sambalpur and Rairakhol on the Cuttack road on 17th/18th November 1857. Since the British forces were frequently becoming sick during operations in the jungle areas of Sambalpur and there was lack of proper medical facilities in Sambalpur, the Principal Assistant Commissioner wrote to the Commissioner, Cuttack to send some medical men to Sambalpur[27]. Accordingly, two doctors Dr. T. Moore and Dr. D. Hanson, from Ganjam accompanied by a corps of sebundies were despatched to Sambalpur. On 15 November, the Principal Assistant Commissioner, Sambalpur despatched to *sowars* (horse men) and two attendants (*sayees*) to escort them to Sambalpur. The party were warned of dangers from the rebels by the king of Rairakhol at Rampur. Dr. Moore sent a letter to Sambalpur to send some more military men with two *sayees*, one for him and the other for Dr. Hanson. Accordingly 25 *sebundies* were sent to Rampur[28].

On 18 November, the two *sayees*, sent on 15 November, came back to Sambalpur and reported to the Principal Assistant Commissioner that they were captured by the rebels but the two managed to escape. Further they told that they had learnt about the escape of the two doctors while their personal effects had been looted The *sowars* with them were also set free on 19th but their horses, arms and belongings were taken away by the rebels. None of them was physically harmed, which indicates that the rebels did not intend to harm their countrymen in the service of the British Government.

The Principal Assistant Commissioner Cap. Leigh became perturbed to learn about all that, particularly the safety of the two medical men. He decided to proceed personally to Jujomora on 20th morning. With great difficulty he reached Jujomora and, there he learnt that Dr. Moore was slain. He met Dr. Hanson at Charmal near Jujomora. Dr. Hanson[29] told him that he had a narrow escape while one of his *palkee* bearers died from a shot and the other three fled away. He ran away into jungles to save his life. He returned to Jujomora at 7 O'Clock in the morning of 18th. Then he proceeded to Charmal camp amidst *sepoys* whom he happened to see where he learnt the death of Dr. Moore. He was hotly pursued by the rebels. A skirmish took place between the rebels and the *sepoys* for sometime after which the rebels fled to the jungles. At Rampur, Dr. Moore's bearer reported Leigh that while he was following him (Dr. Hanson), he was surrounded by about 40 men. They asked his bearers to go away leaving him alone. Despite Dr. Moore's remonstrations, he was cut to pieces with a sword. Two of his bearers were also killed and one was injured.

While returning to Sambalpur on 25 November, Cap. Leigh and his advance guards of the Ramgarh Battalion were fired at the Badpati Pass by some rebels from behind heaps of stones. He went up the hill with a few of the Madras *sepoys*, but the rebels fled away. Two *Sepoys* were killed on the spot and one of wounds while three were seriously injured.

The whole country in the vicinity of Sambalpur was in the control of the rebels who were posted in group in every three/four miles. They were firing at Government pickets. The *dak* (postal) communication between Sambalpur and Cuttack had practically been stopped, so that no information about the developments could be sent to the Commissioner, Cuttack. He got the piece of news of Dr.Moore's death as late as 23 November at his Angul camp.

The developments weighed heavily on the mind of Cap. Leigh. He wrote to Cap. E.J. Dalton, the Officiating Commissioner of Chhotanagpur that 'the melancholy occurrence' of Dr. Moore's death added to his great anxiety. He felt as if 'he should become demented'. His nervousness may be realised from his own words:

> There are only three boys (British soldiers) in the troops and all rests on me. If you manage to come in this direction, how thankful I would be, for I feel that the settlement of this district is beyond any powers and the difficulties seem to be increasing every day[30].

The incident has been observed as: it 'could not be considered a calculated move on the part of the leaders and far less Surendra Sai ….. It could be the result of "mob-frenzy". Nonetheless, such incidents were fanned by the *Gauntias* and *Garhtteas* who had either lost their land or taxed for it which they had been enjoying since the times of the *Rajahas*. Madhu Gauntia of Luisingh had been suspected of his involvement in the incident.

Two days later (on 3 December 1857) Cap. Leigh wrote another letter to Cap. Dalton about the prevailing situation as follows:

> Things are looking very bad here. The Cuttack-Raipur/Bombay mail has been stopped on the Raipur road.

Two of the Dak houses burnt and two wallets partially destroyed. Great sickness prevailed among troops, there is rarely any medicine for them and worst of all an unwilling spirit is beginning to show itself among some of the sepoys. The Cuttack Dak is also stopped. I know not how it will all end and the anxiety I suffer, is more than I can express. The sepoys seem to have got quite fear-stricken[31].

Sambalpur (November-December 1857)

The two-month-long time, i.e., from 31 October to the middle of December 1857 was one of anarchy at Sambalpur. People were so much panic-stricken that members of staff of offices did not go to do their duty, courts remained empty as parties did not arrive, revenue could not be collected, mails could not be despatched or received, many people left home and hearth for other places and, importantly, insurgents made surprise attacks on British troops and harassed them. Sickness among the troops in the inhospitable areas of operation, non-availability of adequate medical services and medicine had demoralizing effect on the troops.

Cockburn, the Commissioner of Cuttack realised the gravity of the situation in Sambalpur and decided to send reinforcements to strengthen the defence and restore confidence of the people there. He instructed Major Bates, the Officer Commanding, Cuttack to send a few efficient officers to Sambalpur. Cap. Woodbridge and Lt. Vallance were sent with forces and they reached Sambalpur on 3rd December 1857. Cap. Sweeney of 32nd Madras Native Infantry (MNI) who was on the way to join the regiment at Kamptee was asked to report for duty at Sambalpur. Maj. Bates proceeded with two companies of MNI while on 15 December Cockburn sent another two Companies. Lt. Macneil, the Agent of Orissa Hill Tracts sent Cap. Dyer with 581

Ghumsar men who were "peculiarly suited for jungle warfare". Cap. E.G. Wood from Nagpur arrived with a corps of Cavalry. Cockburn was virtually in charge of the law and order situation of Sambalpur District, which was then under Chhotnagpur division, from the beginning of December. In the mean time, it was considered difficult to control Sambalpur from Chhotanagpur and transferred to Orissa Division on 19 December.

After taking over charge of Sambalpur J.F. Cockburn decided to act vigorously. He proceeded to Sambalpur with a force of Madras artillery under Cap. Elwyn and one contingent of MNI under Maj. Wyndham to direct operations. The party was attacked by the rebels on many occasions but they managed to reach Sambalpur on 20 January 1858.

In the mean time, on 17 December 1857, Leigh, the Senior Assistant Commissioner, Sambalpur proceeded to attack rebels, who were reported to be there in the jungles about 4 miles from Sambalpur Cantonment, with an army comprising 100 men of 40 MNI, one detachment of mountain howitzers, 30 persons of Ramgarh Battalion under the command of Harinath Singh Jamadar. The rebels took positions behind a barricade of stones. Since penetration into the jungles was difficult, the army had charged some shells and were returning. The rebels started chasing them and clashes took place for some time. Finally, the rebels retreated into the jungles losing four of them[32].

Operations Began : Battle of Kudopali

The increase of the strength of the army – there being 6 companies of 40 MNI consisting of 420 men, 2 companies of 5th MNI, one troop of Ramgarh Battalion, 25 *sebundies*, 50 *Paiks*, a troop of artillery men with four howitzer guns emboldened the SAC Sambalpur, Leigh to begin fresh assaults on the rebels. Cap. E.G. Wood and a force of 150 men of 40th MNI, 75 men of Nagpur Irregular Cavalry and 50 men of Ramgarh Battalion, Leigh left for Kudopali near Papanga hill (Bheden) where he heard the rebels had gathered. The plan and the route of the advancing army were kept secret. They left Sambalpur at 3 A.M. 30 December 2857 and by daybreak they were there. The rebels were taken by surprise.

Instead of launching attacks on them, Cap. E.G. Wood pretended retreating so as to induce the rebels to chase them to the plains. The rebels could not see through the tricks of the enemy and chased them to the village below the hill. As to the battle, as revealed from Leigh's report to Dalton[33], Commissioner, Chhotanagpur, Cap. Wood charged the rebels with his *sowars*, killing three in his own hands. The Cavalry charged from all directions followed by charges of Infantry. 53 of rebels were said to have been killed while many of the rest took to flight leaving behind matchlocks, weapons and rations. The principal rebel Surendra Sai who was said to be there could not be traced. The greatest loss, however, was the murder of Chhabil Sai, the fifth brother of Surendra. While he was running in the village's street to catch his horse, shots hit his back and he succumbed to the injuries. Eleven were captured of whom four were hanged to death, two were sentenced to rigorous imprisonment for 7 years and the rest were freed for want of evidence against them[34].

Chhabila was killed but continued to live in the memory of the people. The village girls of the area preserve the memory of his death through their songs. Of late, a statue of the hero has been raised in the village and functions are organized every

year. He has been given the honour of a martyr by the people. A Dash writes:

> This was the first great victory of the Government over the rebels and they were encouraged by the incident in their future line of action. It was such a victory that the news was sent to Calcutta by wire from Madras[35].

References

1. *Veer Surendra*, pp. 135-6.

2. *Surendra Sai,* p. 94.

3. *ibid,* p. 83.

4. Appendix-I, *Balangir District Gazetteer* (ed. Senapati, N., Bhubaneswar, 1964).

4a. *ibid.*

5. *Veer Surendra*, p. 145.

6. *ibid*, p. 140.

7. Senior Assistant Commissioner, Sambalpur to   Cap. Dalton, Officiating Commissioner, Hazaribag letter No. 50 dat3ed 19 September, 1857.

8. *Surendra Sai*, p. 98.

9. Letter No.50 dated 19 September 1852.

10. *ibid.*

11. *Veer Surendra*, p. 141.

12. Letter No. 527 dated 2.10.1857 from Cap. Leigh to Commissioner, Chhotanagpur.

12a. *Veer Surendra*, p. 139.

12b. *ibid,* pp. 134-35.

13. L.S.S. O Malley and F.C. King : *Bihar and Orissa District Gazetteer, Sambalpur*, p. 35.

13a.   Letter dt. 13.8.1857 from Leigh to Cuttack Commissioner & Letter

No. 43 dt. 22.8.1857 from Leigh to Commissioner, Chhotanagpur.

14.   Letter No. Nil dt. 6 October 1857 from Leigh to Cap. Dalton.

15.   Letter No. 242 dt. 30.10.1857.

16.   *ibid.*

17.   Letter No.68 dt. 24 October 1857 from Cap. Leigh to Cap. Dalton.

18.   *Surendra Sai*, p. 104.

19.   Letter No. 224 (Political) dt. 12 November 1857.

20.   Commissioner, Cuttack to Government of Bengal, Letter No. 294 dt. 30.11.1857.

21.   Commissioner, Cuttack to Secretary, Government of Bengal, Letter No. 318 dt. 5.12.1857.

22.   Letter No. 113 dt. 9 February 1858.

23.   Leigh's letter to Dalton No. 76 dt. 7 November 1857.

24.   Leigh's letter to Dalton No. 86 dt. 23 November 1857.

24a.   *Surendra Sai*, p. 114.

25.   *ibid.*

26.   Letter No. 1 dt. 15 February 1858 from Camp: Pahadsirgida.

27.   The Governor-General moved the Medical board for deputation of the two medical officers in Letter No. 945 dt. 23 October 1857.

28.   Leigh to Dalton from camp : Charmal Letter No. 84 dt. 23 November 1857.

29. Dash, A. *Life of Surendra Sai*, pp. 69-72; Dr. Hanson's statement recorded at Camp : Charmal on 23 November 1857.

30. D.O. No. Nil dt. 1 December 1857.

31. D.O. letter No. Nil dt. 3 December 1857 (Board Proceedings, Judicil, Accn. No. 1857, p. 459).

32. Letter No. 90 dt. 17.12.1857 from Leigh to Dalton.

33. Letter No. 94 dt. 30.12.1857 from Leigh to Dalton.

34. *Guide to Orissa Records,* IV, p. 97.

35. *Life of Surendra Sai,* p. 77.

CHAPTER 4

THE FULLY FLEDGED REBELLION

Extensive Military Operations

The increase of the strength of the army as well as the successes in December 1857 encouraged the British to carry on extensive military operations against the rebels of Sambalpur. Besides, as Commissioner Cockburn has reported to the Secretary, Government of West Bengal "it will be necessary, now that the cold season is on, to take some active steps towards following them (the insurgents) up, wherever they may be collected"[1], and establish few outposts in different parts of the country to maintain law and order and ensure regular *Dak* services between Sambalpur and other places.

The lawlessness was spreading over the length and breadth of Sambalpur district. Harassment of the supporters of the British Government and the army continued unabated. Reports of beating up of police personnels had become a regular affair. Combing operations were becoming difficult due to barricade constructions on the roads, guerrilla fighting of insurgents and support of local people. Among the passes of hills (*ghats*) boulders were tied with creepers at heights of the hills and when forces would pass by that road, the insurgents would cut off the creepers and make boulders roll down, smashing the passing-by troops and barricading the narrow paths. From above the hillocks and behind stone works, arrows would be shot at the army below. It became difficult to encounter the rebels as they remained hidden or would run away after tormenting the combing army or police parties. The informers were given salutary punishment. The people in general were harassed by both Police and army for not giving information about the rebels and, by the rebels if they provided any support or information to the Police or army. In fact, the whole of the district was a picture of a horrible state of lawlessness and disorder. The successes at Kudopali or other places either could not circulate among the people or those were not taken seriously by them. In fact, the incidents could not make any demoralizing effect on the people.

Such a situation could not brook delay for Government action. Commissioner Cockburn, as pointed out earlier wrote to the Secretary of Government of Bengal to establish military outposts at strategic places and to 'defeat, disburse and hunt the rebels down'. A. Dash writes:

> A colossal force had been collected at Sambalpur from all
> possible sources, so much so that Cuttack was left with four
> useless guns without any artillery men to operate them[2].

Operations of 1858 : Kolabira Incident

Maj. Bates, Officer Commanding, Cuttack was sent to Sambalpur. He arrived on 7 January 1858 and assumed the charge of the forces stationed there. He cleared off the Jharghati Pass of the rebels and restored mail communication with Ranchi. He made heavy firing and destroyed the stoneworks of the rebels. Udant Sai who was in charge of the pass ran away with the rebels, many of whom had already been killed, and it fell into the hands of the British army.

Thereafter, Maj. Bates marched to Kolabira, 'a nest of rebels' – a stronghold of the rebels. The *Zamindar* Karunakar Gauntia was a veteran supporter of the principal rebel Surendra Sai. The entire village was besieged and put to fire. The *Gartia* with thirteen rebels surrendered. His *Zamindari* was confiscated and he was hanged at Sambalpur on 11 February 1858[3].

Capt. Shakespeare who came from Raipur with a squadron of cavalry had a success against the rebels at Singhora pass and restored mail communication with Raipur. However, after his return the pass was reoccupied by the rebels. The pass was vitally important for both the rebels and the army, situated as it was on Sambalpur-Nagpur as well as Calcutta-Bombay lines. The control over it by one party could give success to it against the other. Its interception by rebels would cut off the line of communication for transportation of army and *dak*. So it was very strongly fortified and guarded by the veteran *Zamindar* of Ghens Madho Singh and his son Hatte (Hathi) Singh. Eleven of the rebel-fighters died of the firing by Shakespeare's cavalry and, Hatte was severely injured and carried away to a safe place by his followers. However, Shakespeare could not stay long at the pass after his victory to consolidate the gains. Hardly had he returned to Raipur, Suredra Sai recaptured the pass and reorganized its defensive position under Kunjel Singh and Bairi Singh – two other members of the Ghens *Zamindar* family.

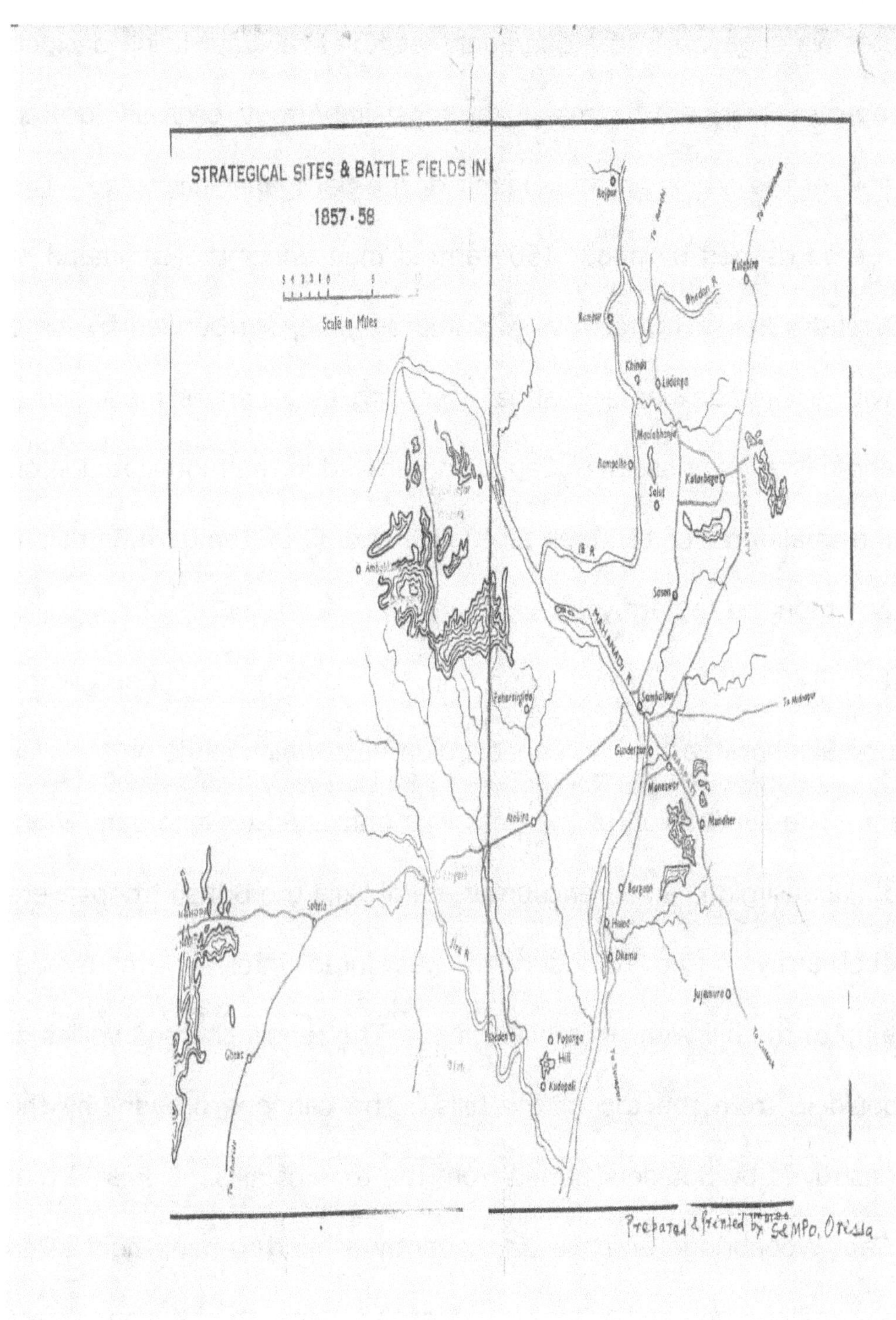

Attack on Debrigarh and Pahadsirgida : Death of Cap. Woodbridge

When Maj. Bates ws engaged in the operations at Kolabira, Cap. Leigh decided to launch an attack against Debrigarh fortress – the most important, centrally located and strategic stronghold of the rebels on the summit of the Barapahar hill range. The fortress was said to be garrisoned by about 1500 armed men under the command of the principal rebel Surendra Sai. The fortress was impregnable, surrounded by huge natural stone walls with a cascade named Kandajor serving as a sort of moat and a number of hideouts and passages of escape. Cap. Leigh arrived in the foothill region on 14 January 1858 with a small force of 150 men of 40 MNI and 30 of Ramgarh Battalion. The rebels attacked and repulsed the army[4].

On 12 February, 1858 a big army under Cap. Woodbridge and Cap. Wood proceeded to re-occupy Singhora Pass. The Pahadsirgida Pass which came on the way was attacked by them. The supervision of the pass was entrusted to Janardan Singh, the rebel *Zamindar* of Pahadsirgida. In an encounter at Poblikila the British troops were defeated by the rebel army. Cap. Woodbridge was lured into an ambuscade. Desperately, he rode up to the hill with his artillery men. The rebels charged vollies of missiles and huge boulders from the top of the hills. The cannons brought by the British troops were destroyed by boulders hurled from the tops of hills. It is said that the rebels came to Cap. Woodbridge and the *Zamindar* by a hand-to-hand fight killed Cap. Woodbridge. The artillery men and other *Sepoys* of the Ramgarh battalion, except two who were severely injured, were slain. The report of the disaster, not the death of Woodbridge which was discovered later, reached Sambalpur.

Ensign Warlow attacked Paharsirgida pass on 14 February 1858. He divided his troops into three parties – two flanking parties to proceed by left and right and an advancing party in the middle for a frontal encounter with the rebels. The rebels could know the strength of the enemy and the tactics of surrounding them. They found that they could not cope with the British forces and ran away into the surrounding jungles. It was Warlow who discovered the body of Cap. Woodbridge with the head cut off and chopped[5].

The encounters at Pahadirghida revealed that the rebels' fighting spirit had not dampened after the Papanga hill (Kudopali) incidents. The rebels' forces were still forceful, despite setbacks at some quarters.They were ready to fight more battles. Cap. Nicholes reached Debrigarh when the rebels fled away. Major Wyndham won some successes. Cap. Dyer of the Ghumsar troops and the Paik forces destroyed some villages around Sambalpur, which were supposed to be shelters of insurgents.

Cockburn, the Commissioner wrote:

> Heat of the jungles after March becomes intense and marching at night becomes unwholesome, so the real safe time is only from December to March, four months. The British troops at Sambalpur would like to waste no time and, therefore prepared to crush the rebellion before the advent of the hot season. Being driven from all directions due to combing process undertaken by the army the activists among them retired to their fortress, and consequent upon a combined attack, the insurgents fled into the inaccessible jungles and hills[6].

Other Measures of Cockburn

Besides vigorous military action, other stern measures of Cockburn brought in a critical period for the rebels. The rebels were hunted at their stations and strongholds and found no respite. Two factors, however, were favourable to the rebels. The revolution was gradually spreading over to the surrounding Native States of Sambalpur Tract and the adjacent *Zamindaris* of present Chhatisgarh State. Those two not only harassed the British Government but also helped to the rebellion to continue for three/four years more. Rebel leaders, in the knowledge and with the tacit support of Ruling Chiefs of Patana, Khariar and Bamra etc., were active to canvass support among people in general and tribal people in particular. For example, Ujjal Sai – Surendra Sai's brother was gathering support of the people of Patna State. Hira Vajradhar Dev, the ruling Chief, abetted his activities. For his failure to arrest Ujjal, he was fined Rs. 1000/- by Commissioner Cockburn.

To all those, the land settlement at Sambalpur added fuel to the fire of rebellion. It has been observed:

> The settlement of the land tenure, which was basic to the factor of dissaffection could not be handled. The people felt the continuance of the foreign rule was the antithesis to the solution of their demands. These demands were the restitution of their rights to land, the restoration of the villages granted by the Chauhan rulers, to the deities and the supreme goddess Samaleswari. The Brahmins continued to guide the peoples with their intellectual and religious propaganda[7].

It may be pointed out that the deities in silence and the Brahmins behind the scene, as it were, 'guided the people'. As it has been pointed out in the previous Chapter, rent-free lands known as *Devottar* and *Brahmottar* had been granted by various kings in favour of deities and Brahmins. In the case of tribal deities, which at one time included the premier deity Samaleswari – before it was made the State Deity (*Rastra-Devata*) by the first Chauhan King, whether in the capital or in the villages they were granted with rent free land for their worship and maintenance of temples. The village priests or *Jhankars* of small temples were tribal people while in the cases of bigger temples or those of the Hindu pantheon Brahmins, as in the case of Huma Siva temple or Gopalji temple of Sambalpur were also granted lands for the services to the deities or other services which were known as *Brahmlottar*. When such land grants were revoked or taxed by the British Government not only the worshippers, whether tribal or Brahmin, were affected but also the daily rituals and festivals associated with the deities were dislocated or came to a stop. As a result, the socio-religious set up was in a state of topsy-turvy. There were as many as 62 villages which paid 844 *Tankas* - 1 *anna* – 6 *pies* to support Brahmins and 37 villages which supported temples with 634 *Tankas* 10 *anna* and 9 *pies* as recorded by H.B. Impey, the Deputy Commissioner of Sambalpur. Besides, there were various kinds of village servants, viz., Jhankar, *Ganda* (Chawkidar or Watch-man), *Nariha* (Water-carrier), *Negi* (Clerk or writer) *Kumbhar* (potter), *Lohar* (blacksmith), *Bhandari* (Barber) and *Dhoba* (washer man) as pointed out by Hamid Settlement Report[8]. The 1854 Settlement, as hinted in the previous Chapter, was rather 'perfunctory in nature and there were considerable shortcomings in the operations', and further 'distasteful' for the enhancement of revenue that was imposed on such lands.

Thus all classes – *Zamindars, Gauntias, Garhtteas*, village priests and servants and Brahmins were coming closer to one another by such circumstances. The tribals of them had the fighting and resisting spirit but they lacked leadership which was provided by the feudal lords like *Zamindars/Gauntias* etc. The Brahmins – the respectable caste of the society – who were intelligent, as hinted above, through their religious propaganda against the British fanned, disaffection among the people. It is evident from the involvement of a few eminent Brahmins in the Rebellion like Mrityunjaya Panigrahi, Padmanabh Guru, Ganesh Ram Upadhyaya and his two sons, Dharnidhar Mishra, Jagabandhu Hota, Loknath Panda etc. Thus cutting across lines of caste and socio-economic status, people made a common cause against the Government and came into the fray of Rebellion.

During his short stay at Sambalpur, Cockburn, the Commissioner of Cuttack took all possible steps to suppress the Rebellion. The Ruling Chiefs, the *Zamindars*, the *Garhtteas,* the *Gauntias* were warned against extending any sort of support to the rebels. Some of them like King of Patna were fined for their inability to arrest rebels. The *Zamindar* of Kharsal, Diyal Sardar was hanged on 3 March 1858. The *Zamindaris* of Ghens, Kolabiria, Lakhanpur, Bheden, Kharsal, Patkulunda, Loisingh, Kodabaga and Kurkut were confiscated[9]. Madhu *Gauntia* of Jujomora who was considered as involved in the murder of Dr. Moore was also executed. Three central military stations were set up on the roads to Nagpur, Cuttack and Calcutta from Sambalpur manned by military personnel. Eleven outposts were set up in different parts of the districts, each with twenty-five *Sepoys* of the Ramgarh Battalion. Thus his measures had gone a long way to weaken the Rebellion and thereby enhanced the prestige of the Government in the District. Law and order was restored to a great extent before he left Sambalpur in the last part of March 1858.

Forster as Deputy Commissioner

Capt. W.R. Forster took over charge of Deputy Commissioner, Sambalpur from Cap. Leigh on 27 March 1858. He was vested with both civil and military powers for the district which was declared a disturbed area. He was a strong man and came with the avowed objective of 'to free the country from disaffection and insurgency', after earning encomium for suppressing the rebellion of Porahat. Things took a different turn. His administration was marked by 'fiendish cruelty' to rebels and rough-and-tough behaviour towards Ruling chiefs and *Zamindars* of the Tract. The insurgents on their part were not relenting or submissive. They resorted to retaliation. Thus 'The revolution in Sambalpur from April 1858 was more severe and methodical butultimately the mighty British force had to bow down before it'[10].

The extinction of the fire of rebellion by the middle of 1858, in different parts of the country, the taking over of administration of East India Company by Her Majesty's Government of England in November 1858 had a little impact on Sambalpur. Both the parties – the British and the insurgents or the people were ready to act. If Forster was stern and rough, the people were ready to face all tribulations and sufferings. A serious turn came in the rebellion from 1858 April.

Forster's policy of weakening the rebels by keeping away the Ruling chiefs and *Zamindars* from rendering any help and, thereby crippling the resources of the rebels was successful to some extent. Secondly, he unleashed a reign of terror for the people.

Large scale arrests, mock trial and severe punishment became the order of the day. Flogging to innocent people was also adopted.

In April 1858, Forster convened a Conference and invited the Ruling Chiefs and *Zamindars* and urged them not to extend any help to the rebels and help the Government to capture them. The ruler of Rairakhol in the meantime had captured Madhu Gauntia and handed over him to the Government in connection with the murder of Dr. Moore. The Patna ruler Hira Vajradhar after the Conference handed over Ujjal Sai who the ruler had given shelter and support in his State. Ujjal was hanged on 1 June 1858 by orders of Forster[11]. The Patna king was remitted of fine Rs. 1000/- imposed on him a little earlier by Cockburn. The king of Sarangarh promised to be loyal to British Government.

Forster's actions continued in full swing thereafter. Towards close of 1858, Forster decided to make a surprise attack on a *Zamindar* whose members of family had become famous for their sufferings and sacrifices in the annals of history. It was the Ghens *Zamindar* family. The old, veteran *Zamindar* Madho Singh was captured and hanged at Sambalpur in December 1858. He attacked Bheden whose *Zamindar* Manohar Singh died while fighting.

Sambalpur jail overflowed with inmates. About 300 convicts were interned in the cells meant for accommodation of 90. The flogging of some prisoners was considered illegal by Cockburn and that was withdrawn. All those were done to terrify people to not to sympathize and support the rebels.

Throughout 1859, elaborate and severe military operations were carried on throughout Sambalpur district. Forster tried his best to capture Surendra Sai, the principal rebel leader who was at large, whose whereabouts could not be known. It was said that he had left Sambalpur and was seeking support of people and chiefs in the surrounding states and *Zamindaris.*

As a result of vigorous military operations of Cap. Forster, the insurgents found it difficult to continue their activities from the old bases of Debrigarh, Jharghati, Badpati and Singhora. Their resources, arms and weapons, fighters were also dwindling. So the principal rebel leaders decided to shift their bases to peripheral and adjacent territories. It was reported that they were collecting both manpower and money in Rewa State of C.P. from a camp in the village Koderee Kodar[13]. The *Zamindar* of Pendra informed the Deputy Commissioner of Raipur that two local leaders Runwant Singh and Guru Singh were instigating the *Malguzars* of Sohagpur *Taluq* to support the rebels leaders of Sambalpur. The Deputy Commissioner of Sambalpur was informed about the activities of the rebels[14]. The rebels spent the entire year 1859 "on consolidation of fresh strength over a vastly extensive area from Surguja to Khariar and Bindra-Nawagarh and even beyond that to Junagarh (Kalahandi district) and Jeypore (Koraput district) hill tracts"[15].

Role of Peripheral Regions

The rebels adopted the strategy of attacking and terrifying the supporters of the British rather than confronting the British army at that stage when their resources and man power were depleted. They shifted their bases of operation to peripheral regions.

They started constructing some amount of defence in some strategic places on the border region of Raipur and Sambalpur, particularly in the Jonk river valley (present Nawapara district located amidst dangerous hills, forests and rapids.

The Deori Incident

The first attack of the Sambalpur rebels was directed against Maharaja Sai, the *Binjhal Zamindar* of Deoree, situated about one hundred miles east of Raipur. The attack was conducted in broad day-light on 16th July 1860. It may be recalled that in November 1857 Maharaja Sai, the *Zamindar* of Deori rendered valuable help to Lt. Lucie Smith to capture his uncle Naryan Singh, the patriotic *Zamindar* of Sonakhan (Chhatisgarh) who was executed in December 1857 on the charge of rebellion. The family members of Narayan Singh, including his son Govind Singh, were also captured and detained at Nagpur. Subsequently they were released but kept under the surveillance of Maharaja Sai who obtained the *Zamindari* of Sonakhan on the condition of a limited lease. Govind Singh was sincerely bent upon wreaking vengeance on him. He married the daughter of Kunjal Singh, the rebel *Zamindar* of Ghens and acted as one of the trusted followers of Surendra Sai. Govind Singh had two faithful men – Pahar Singh and Rajee Ghasia who kept Surendra Sai informed about the treacherous conduct of the Deoree *Zamindar* who acted as British agent.

On 16th July about five hundred rebels under the command of Kunjal Singh and Govind Singh marched against Deoree and besieged the house of Maharaja Sai just at noon of the day. They broke open the doors and rushed into the house. Govind Singh pulled the *Zamindar* out and stabbed him furiously while Kunjal Singh cut off his head.

The house of the *Zamindar* was ransacked and all the valuables were taken away by the rebels. They attacked some other villages of the *Zamindari* to punish the supporters of the British and returned to Kholagarh in Khariar[16].

Capt. Forster, the Officiating Commissioner of Sambalpur, issued *parwana* to the Raja of Khariar to apprehend the rebels and not to allow them shelter in his territory. He also issued *parwans* to the Rajas of Patna, Borasambar, Bindra Nuagarh, Phuljhar and Sarangarh to help the Government in capturing the rebels. He sent contingents of troops to suppress them. After the Deoree incident troops were mobilized from Sambalpur as well as from Nagpur. Lt. Taylor who commanded the troops from Sambalpur was instructed by Capt. Forster to capture Surendra Sai, Govind Singh and Kunjal Singh. Major E.K. Elliot, the Commissioner of Nagpur declared rewards of five hundred and two hundred fifty rupees for the capture of Govind Singh and Kunjal Singh respectively.

Raid on Khullari

Another raid was conducted by the rebels in the night of 24th August 1860 against two villages, Timroda and Brindaban in the Khullaree Parganna of Raipur as those two places were reported to be the seats of conspiracy against the rebels. Large bands of rebels, whose number could not be ascertained, led by Surendra Sai and Kunjal Singh, crossed the river Jonk in the night and marched to the Khullaree hills wherefrom they dashed against the two villages. A number of persons were killed and wounded and after a short scuffle with the rebels the inhabitants of both the villages took to flight in panic.

The incident was reported on the 26th August by Cap. C. Elliot, Deputy Commissioner of Raipur, to the Commissioner of Nagpur[17]. The former requested the latter to send a large force of Cavalry and infantry to undertake operation against the rebels. The Commissioner of Cuttack Cockburn, who was then at Raipur on leave, proceeded towards the Khullaree Parganna with two Companies of Infantry Battalion but failed to achieve any success because of the difficult terrain and unhealthy climate. He could not withstand the heavy exertions of the operations and fell seriously ill. A large number of his men also suffered from sickness in the inhospitable hilly zone and the detachments were soon withdrawn. A levy of *Beldars* was posted in the Khullaree Parganna to guard the frontier area against the infiltration of the rebels. Major Forster directed Lt. Taylor to march towards the Manikgarh hill in the Upper Jonk valley through Borasambar and he himself started for Khariar to put pressure on the *Raja* to render help and supply provisions to the troops of Lt. Taylor. But the campaigns ended in total failure as no trace of Surendra Sai and his party could be detected from any source.

Manikgarh and Tanwat *Zamindari* of Khariar

Manikgarh was located in the *Zamindari* of Tanwat of Khariar State. Lal Sah the *Zamindar* of that estate was a loyal follower of Surendra Sai and was deadly against those who supported the cause of the British. During the attack against the Deoree *Zamindari*, Lal Sah helped Govind Singh and Kunjal Singh with men and money and he took all possible care to accommodate the rebels in the Manikgarh hills and provided security and logistic facilities to the rebels. Surendra Sai directed him to command a party of rebels against the village Pursudde in Ferringeswar *Zamindari* of Raipur as that village was also a stronghold of the supporters of the British. Lal Sah led a large troop of armed men and descended down the hills on the 4th September 1860. The village Pursudde was looted and a number of people were killed[18].

Lal Sah knew that his activities in support of the rebels and his attack of the villages on the borders of Raipur would not go unheeded and sooner or later he would be taken to task by the British. He pretended to be a supporter of the British and sent two of his men to the camp of Lt. Cockburn with the message that he could catch hold of both Surendtra Sai and Govind Singh who were taking shelter inside his *Zamindari* provided the British would repose trust on him and forgive him for his past actions. Cockburn knew well that Lal Sah was a notorious rebel and that he was involved in plunder and murder in several villages where the people did not support the revolution. Despite of that he recommended the offer to the Deputy Commissioner of Raipur as it involved very important issue[19].

The Deputy Commissioner of Raipur wanted to know the opinion of Capt. Forster the Officiating Commissioner of Sambalpur about Lal Shah as both of them were jointly campaigning against Surendra Sai. Forster had already written to him on 21st September that the *Tahnoot* man was not to be relied upon and that he might have sent his 'ambassadors' to Cockburn to have an idea of the British army camp and assess the strength of the British force. However, he wrote that it was worthwhile to seize the opportunity of getting the support of the *Zamindar* who should be told that his rebellious activities would be overlooked if he could capture Surendra Sai and Govind Singh. He further stated that Government's e declaration of reward of Rs. 1000 and Rs.

500 for the capture of Surendra Sai and Govind Singh respectively should be made widely public. As such, any person who would help Government by rendering that commendable service would receive the rewards. The Tahnoot *Zamindar,* although a miscreant and of doubtful integrity, there was no harm if he may be tried 'out of political expediency'[20].

It is revealed from the letter of Forster that Surendra Sai and Govind Singh were then recruiting followers from among the tribal people of Jeypore (Koraput) and the adjoining Bastar *Elaka* and they were trying to make their revolution deep rooted and diffused over a large area. He had, however, made sufficient military arrangements to restrain the activities of the rebels on Sambalpur side. A strong party of Sebundies was stationed at Bhaingrajpur in Borasambar and the detachment of Lt. Taylor was camping at Sankre in Phuljhar while the troops of Lt. Cockburn were guarding the Raipur frontier. Capt. Forster sent further reinforcement from Sambalpur to strengthen the party of Lt. Taylor in Phuljhar[21].

Regarding the offer of the Tahnoot *Zamindar,* it is known that the Lieutenant Governor of Bengal recommended the proposal for consideration of His Excellency the Governor General-in-Council[22] and it was examined at length in the Foreign Department. The Governor General accepted the recommendation of Capt. Forster and passed order for its circulation. The orders were communicated to the Government of Bengal[23], but the *Zamindar* of Tahnoot whose offer was nothing more than a pretence never acted according to his promise.

Manikgarh as the base of the Rebels

In the early part of 1860 Manikgarh on the hill range in the Upper Jonk river basin near Nawapara was the stronghold of the rebels. The eminent leaders like Surendra Sai, Kamal Singh, Hatte Singh, Kunjal Singh etc. remained there. The place was located amidst mountains and forests and nature of the terrain made it difficult for the British military operations for lack of communication, inhospitable climate and, more importantly, amidst hostile inhabitants of the region. Secondly, the fortress was at a strategic point commanding supervision on both Sambalpur and Raipur zones. It was at the cross-roads of West Orissa and Chhatisgarh which could provide them with logistic support from the people, the *Zamindars* and the kings of the surrounding regions. Thus, safety and security to their hide-outs and supervision over surrounding zones were made available to the rebels at that place.

Both Forster, Officiating Commissioner of Sambalpur and C. Eliot, Deputy Commissioner of Raipur were of the view that large scale military operation was the need of the time in Manikgarh area. Both of them requested the authorities of Nagpur to send a large force of cavalry and infantry for the purpose.

Patna State

The rebels not only attacked and terrorized the village headmen and the *Zamindars* who sided with the British, but also created troubles for the feudatory Rajas who did not support them or gave support to the British. After the betrayal of Ujjal Sai by the Raja of Patna, the Khonds inside his State were incited to rise against the Raja, while the rebels continually invaded the Patna territory and gave no respite to the ruler. Surendra Sai is said to have sent two threatening letters on palm leaves to Raja Hira

Bajradhardeva who, in his turn, submitted those letters to the Deputy Commissioner, Sambalpur out of fear. He complained that his territory was frequently being invaded by the rebels[24].

Bamra

The Raja of Bamra, Braja Sundardeva wrote that he was prepared to render his services either to fight and capture Surendra Sai or to compromise matters with him, whatever was desired by the Government[25]. He assured Forster, the Officiating Commissioner of Sambalpur of his sincere loyalty and thereby incurred great disaffection of the rebels. The Bamra territory was, therefore, frequently invaded by the rebels who resorted to loot, arson and murder and allowed no peace for the Raja. In fact, the Raja himself was once imprisoned by the rebels and was ultimately set free by the intervention of Surendra Sai who extorted from him the promise of support and sympathy for the cause of revolution.

It was by that time that an enquiry was being conducted by the Government of Bengal regarding the conduct of the Rajas to ascertain whether they were giving refuge to the rebels and were guilty of disloyalty towards the authorities. It was observed by the Officiating Principal Assistant Commissioner of Sambalpur that the Raja of Bamra had sympathy for the revolution of Surendra Sai and that his *Paiks* were invading the villages of the British territory. It was pointed out that the *paiks* of Bamara had three times in the past few weeks been "found levying black mail on the Khalsa villages" and the Assistant Commissioner was of the view that the Raja was guilty of gross misconduct. So the Commissioner of Cuttack recommended to the Government of

Bengal that since the Bamra *Raja* was unable to control his own *Paiks* he should be called upon to contribute to the expenses of a Police force which might maintain discipline among the *Paiks* and protect the people from the insurgents' lawless activities[26].

Loknath Mohanty, the Native Agent of the British Government at Banai, reported to Capt. Birch, Deputy Commissioner of Singhbhum, that Surendra Sai had gathered a large force at Sagra on the borders of Gangpur and Bamra and that the plan of the rebels was not only to plunder and murder the well-intentioned people in those two States but also to carry depredations towards Singhbhum[27]. As a precautionary measure, detachments of the Bengal Police Battallion were posted on the confines of Singhbhum and Chaibasa[28]. However, the territory of Bamra suffered from the plundering raids of the rebels which the Raja failed to check effectively.

However Capt. E.T. Dalton, the Commissioner of Chhotanagpur and Capt. Birch, the Deputy Commissioner of Singhbhum were of the view that the Raja of Bamra was loyal to the British Government. In his report to the Secretary to the Government of Bengal, Birch wrote,

> The Bamra Raja was again an instance of neglect which had been shown towards that Chief, descended from a family which had always shown themselves well disposed towards us and consistently loyal throughout the disturbance, he had suffered more than any one else, in consequence his *royats* had been either ruined by the rapacity of the *Budmashes* or harassed to the last by the calls made on them to supply the troops, which have from time to time been sent to Bamorah and the Rajah himself was once made prisoner by Sarunda Sahoo and a body of Mutineers, yet not the slightest encouragement had been afforded, nor any hopes of compensations held out to him. The Raja of Raigarh, I

> believe is another instance of the same kind. I hope this injustice has only to be brought forward to be at once remedied[29].

Raigarh-Sarangarh

The territories of Raigarh and Sarangarh also became the victims of frequent depredations by the rebels after the Chiefs of those two States professed open loyalty to the British. Capt. Birch drew the attention of the Commissioner of Cuttack towards the trouble and agony of the Chief of Raigarh along with those of the Raja of Bamra. The Raja of Sarangarh made several appeals to the British Government for armed assistance and in one of his petitions he stated that the rebels had been making inroads into his territory from the Ambabhona hill tract in Sambalpur district, burning and plundering villages and cutting the noses of women. No satisfactory help could be given to the *Garjat* Chiefs to protect their territories from the widespread attack of the rebels, as large part of the troops had been posted at strategic places of Phuljhar, Borasambar and Khariar, as well as, the Raipur border to check the main onslaught of the rebels. Of the remaining troops at Sambalpur, a large number of them were seriously ailing. The Commissioner of Cuttack pressed upon the Government of Bengal to protect the loyal tributary chiefs[30] from the depredations of frebels.

The British administrators were, however, satisfied with the change of situation in the Garjat States where the Chiefs could no longer be suspected of secretly supporting the insurgents, , as they were on the other hand, being frequently attacked and oppressed by the rebels. The situation was considered to be a favourable indication. It was believed by the British Government that without the support of the

Rajas, there could not be continuance of the rebellion. Maj H.B. Impey after taking over the charge of Sambalpur as the Deputy Commissioner, observed on this problem as follows:

> "It is worthy of remarks that hitherto the *Garjat* States had enjoyed almost total immunity from the incursions of the Sambalpur rebels. A reversion of feeling on the part of the former towards the latter is gaining ground. The issue of this will be substantially favourable to the restoration of order ultimately, whether the plans of such end be based on pacification or coercion"[31].

Bindra-Nawagarh

The Raja of Bindra Nuagarh was a sincere supporter of Surendra Sai and was inimical towards the British since the very beginning of the revolution in 1857. He was suspected to be responsible for several raids of the Sambalpur rebels on different areas of Raipur district and for the murder of some of the supporters of the British Government. He stopped payment of revenue to the British Government and two British agents – Lokanath Singh and Panchanan Singh – sent by Forster to realize the arrears, failed to extort the dues from him[32]. The *Dewan* of the State, who was the brother of the Raja and the *Zamindar* of Chura, was noted for rebellious activities and was involved in many disturbances in Raipur district. Capt. Forster summoned the Raja's brother thrice, but he did not care for responding to his calls. He openly defied the orders of Lt. Vallance on many occasions[33].

Khariar

The Raja of Bindra Nuagarh was naturally suspected to have given shelter and support to Surendra Sai and his party, Raja Krushna Chandra Singh of Khariar was considered to be more dangerous because he was ostensibly showing his loyalty to the British, while sincerely supporting the cause of rebellion. But he was exposed during the military campaigns of Lt. Vallacne in Khariar whom he rendered little assistance. He even misled Lt. Vallance by declaring that there were no rebels anywhere in his State, and when it was subsequently detected that the Principal rebels had their stronghold at the Manikgarh hill, he stated that the Manikgarh area was under the jurisdiction of the *Zamindar* of Thnoot (Kholagarh) who might have harboured the rebels without his knowledge[34]. Lt. Vallance could not believe that "swarm of rebels headed by notorious rebels could have been located in the comfortable habitation in a *Zaminari* of Khariar without the Raja's sanction or connivance"[35].

Military Operations in Zamindaris of Khariar State

The Deputy Commissioner of Raipur was the first British officer to gather from his spies that Surendra Sai, Govind Singh, Kunjal Singh and Hathi Singh together with their followers and women and children counting 125 souls, were taking shelter in a collection of huts at the foot-hill region of the *Gurrah Pahar* on the borders of Khariar and Bindra-Nuagarh. Major Forster, Deputy Commissioner of Sambalpur took prompt action against the Sambalpur rebels encamping at Manikgarh. He personally proceeded towards the site while he directed Lt. Lucie Smith, Assistant Commissioner of Raipur with a contingent of Beldars from Raipur and Lt. D. Vallance with Sebundi levy from Sambalpur for a surprise attack on Mankgarh in the night of November 6, 1860. The rebels came to resist the army at Trisul Mound[36]. When the defensive stone walls which they had constructed fell down, they ran uphill to more secure hide-out.

A very precisely planned attack was made on the rebels on the morning of November 9, 1860. The rebels decided not to continue confrontation with the army and left in batches, with the women and the children towards different places in the jungle terrain. Researchers consider the retreat of the rebels was an act of strategy, although Cap. Forster loudly declared it as a defeat[37]. Lt. Vallance was deployed at Khariar to take precautionary measures against the activities of the rebels.

In the meantime, the rebels had moved to the surrounding areas of Khariar and Bindra-Nawagarh. The British army burnt a few villages in Khariar and asked the Raja to pursue, seize and if possible, punish the fugitive plunderers. He was further instructed to maintain law and order in his state by maintaining police posts. He was warned that he would be answerable for the misdeeds of the rebels.

After evacuation of the Jonk river valley (Sunabeda plateau) by the British forces, the Sambalpur rebels returned to Manikgarh-Gurrah Pahar region. It was at that time that the Rajas of Khariar and Bindra-Nawagarh helped the rebels to the maximum possible extent despite all warnings and instructions to them by the British Government. Cap. Forster was aware of the mischievous conduct of the Rajas and reported about that to the Government of Bengtal, but he dared not take any action against them except arresting the *Zamindar* of Tanwat with his Dewan, both whom were brought to Sambalpur for detention.

The upper Jonk River Valley of Khariar became the base of operations of the rebels against the British Government. From these they carried on depredations against the Rajas of Patna, Raigarh, Sarangarh, Bamanda and Gangpur who were hostile to the cause of the rebels. Recruits were made to the rebel army from those territories as well. Debrigarh, the main stronghold of the early days of the Rebellion wherefrom they have been ousted in the early phase, was reoccupied under Kamal Singh of Lakhanpur *Zamindari*. Predatory raids were made on border of Raipur. The Deputy Commissioner of Raipur found it difficult to control the situation. The supporters of the rebels were increasing day by day. Partisans of Surendra Sai among office people of Sambalpur were suspected[38]. The high-handed administration of Cap. Forster, his military strategy to curb Rebellion was of no avail. He had to leave office of the Deputy Commissioner of Sambalpur after utter failure in April 1861.

Khariar Again

Raja Krishna Chandra had been a suspect of the British from the beginning despite his valuable services to the British authorities. His failure to attend a meeting of the Chiefs summoned by Major Impey, Deputy Commissioner of Sambalpur on the occasion of the visit of R.N. Shore, Commissioner of Cuttack, for discussion of administrative reforms was seriously viewed. He, the Raja of Patna and *Zamindars* of Borasambar (Padampur sub-division of Bargarh district) as well as those of Bindra-Nawagarh, and Phuljhar in present Chhatisgarh were fined thousand rupees each for their disobedience.

Khariar had to pay a price. R.N. Shore in his letter dated 23 January, 1862 reduced the king's position to that of a *Zamindar* although he was allowed to exercise power of criminal administration. Khariar had to pay more. In 1866, Sir Richard Temple, the Chief Commissioner of the Central Provinces made him a *Zamindar* with the title for his failure to attend the Commissioner's Durbar.   It has rightly been

observed by A. Dash in *Life of Surendra Sai*[38]:

> The worst for the British Government were the Raja of
> Khariar Krishna Chandra Singh and the Raja of Bindra-
> Nawagarh Oomrao Sahi. Our records are full of these two
> Rajas specially. If any credit should be given to Surendra
> Sai and the other rebels, equal credit should be given to
> these Rajas who, in the face of all odds and risks to their
> action, gave shelter to the rebels and financed them,
> supplied rations and cattle. Of all the recalcitrant chiefs of
> States and *Zamindars.* the cases of the Rajas of Bindra-
> Nawagarh and Khariar stood altogether on a different
> footing. In the case of the former, it was almost defiance
> and in the case of the latter, it was a professing of loyalty.
> The conduct of Raja Krishna Chandra Singh of Khariar was
> still worse for the British Government but he was more
> intelligent not to be exposed easily.

As discussed above, different parts of Khariar were veritable asylums of the

rebels. The Raja gave them not only a safety cover but also sufficient time to make

defensive stone walls. He helped them to receive ration and cattle and, importantly,

materials for making arms. He gave shelter to Kunjal Singh, a rebel of Ghens *Zamindar*

family. He gave misleading information to Lt. Vallance during his operation in Khariar.

In a letter dated 24 July 1860 to W.R. Forster, Deputy Commissioner of

Sambalpur the Raipur Deputy Commissioner C. Elliot has mentioned that Tanwat

Zamidnar had supplied men and money to Surendra Sai. Besides the other logistic

support, he helped Surendra and the rebels with safe accommodation in various places

like Manikgarh, Gurrah Pahar, Budharaja, Jumlagarh, Baghghula etc. Under Lal Sai's

leadership, farmers and tribals have fought many a guerrilla warfare against the British.

The British general Cockburn felt helpless, when he was sent against Surendra Sai, to suppress the rebels because of the resistance of the tribal on 10 May 1860.

Baghjhula Pahad

Of all the places, Baghjhula hill in Khariar State was considered to be significant from the standpoints of defence as well as guierilla encounter. The caves in the hill provided security of shelter, the streams flowing by the foot-hill drinking water and the whole area, as it were, was barricaded by dense shrub vegetation cover. By providing such facilities to Surendra Sai and the Sambalpur insurgents against the British, Lal Sai has earned immortal fame as a freedom fighter although his name has remained comparatively unknown to the people at large.

Tandul Pahad

The small hillock is situated not very far from Komna of Khariar (Nawapara district). The plain land amidst the hill was the base of operations of the two brothers, viz. Mehnad Singh and Medini Singh, who were almost unknown among the rebel heroes who have sacrificed themselves to the cause of Sambalpur Rebellion against the British. Traditionally known as 'bahangar' in local dialect, which means dacoit, because they looted the wealthy, they have provided shelter and all sorts of hospitality to Surendra and his associates at their place called 'Bahangar basa' (abode of the dacoits) for long 17 days. They were followers of Lal Sai of Tanwat. They provided the rebels with arms.

Of the 22 men whom the two brothers led against the British on an occasion, 18 became martyrs. During the operation of the British army, when 220 soldiers divided into the three groups, made a surprise attack against Surendra Sai and about 150 rebels residing at Manikgarh – Meghnad fought with great heroism in resisting them and became a martyr. Medini Sai avenged his death by killing about 10 men of the enemy's side.

In a letter No. 14 dated 13.3.1861, R.N. Shore, Commissioner of Cuttack Division has informed the Secretary of the Government of Bengal that Omrao Sai, the ruling chief of Bindra-Nawagarh has provided hospitality to Surendra Sai, Govind Singh (of Sonakhan) and some other rebels.

Thus Nawapara district, its nook and cranny, has played a significant role in the rebellion of Surendra Sai for about five years from 1858 to 1862. The sacrifices of the king, *Zamindars* and the people will remain an unforgettable saga in the history of the country.

In October 1861 Deputy Commissiobner, Raipur wrote to the Deputy Commissioner of Sambalpur that if the Rajas of Khariar and Bindra Nuagarh were sincere they could have easily captured the rebels without extraneous aid. The Zamindars of Chhatisgarh laughed at the idea of those rebels remaining at large even for a day save by the connivance of the landlords in whose estates they had taken shelter. The Deputy Commissioner, Raipur further stated that the previous year (i.e. in 1860) some *ryots* of Khariar offered to capture the rebel leaders provided the Raja allowed them to do so. But the Raja remained indifferent. He urged upon the Deputy Commissioner, Sambalpur that the Chiefs of Khariar and Bindra Nuagarh "who were notoriously disaffected to the State and richly deserved punishment, should be summoned and warned that if Surendra Sai and Co., are not apprehended by a certain date, they would forfeit their estates"[39].

Despite both intensive and extensive military operations of the British, things did not improve for them. The rebels recaptured their strongholds which the British forces could not hold for long after occupation for various reasons like shortage of troops, inhospitable climate and hostile native population etc.. As to the rebels, the hilly and jungle terrain, the sincere support of the *Rajas* of Khariar, Bindra, Nawagarh and *Zamindars* of Tanwat etc. as well as the people encouraged them to carry on their depredations against both the British authorities as well as their loyal *Rajas* like those of Patna, Bamra, Raigarh and Sarangarh.

Sambalpur itself could not remain invulnerable to the rebel attacks. Kamal Singh of the Lakhanpur *Zamindari* with his band of insurgent recaptured the famous base of Debrigarh, while Kunjel Singh and Hatte Singh (of Ghens *Zamindari*) made new bases in Himgir forests and continued their raids on Bamra and Gangpur towards the close of 1860. The rebels were said to have official people in Sambalpur as their supporters while the numbers of sympathizers of the principal rebel leader Surendra Sai were suspected of increasing[40]. Thus, by end of 1860 the Rebellion of the Sambalpur Tract had become widespread and more popular. In the early part of January 1861.The insurgents under Khageswar Dao (of Lakhanpur *Zamindar* family) and one Kewal Singh entered into the villages of Sambalpur where they had been received and greeted by the people and presented them with items of ration. They attacked the supporters of the British in Manpur village. They killed one Tiokka Deo of Kuarmunda who was an informer of the British[41].

The policy of 'blood and iron' of Deputy Commissioner Forster was of no avail to crush the Rebellion. In fact, he was discredited and removed in March 1861.

References

1.	*OJR*, Vol. 126, No. 297, 2 December, 1857.

2.	*Life of Surendra Sai*, p. 78.

3.	*Sambalpur District Gazetteer* (ed) O'Malley, p. 33.

4.	*History of Freedom Movement in Orissa,* II, p. 24.

5.	Barlow's letter No. Nil dated 15.2.1858 from Camp : Pahadsirgida to Officer Commanding Cap. Micoloil; Letter No. 907 dated 6 March, 1858 from A.R. Young, Secretary to Government of Bengal to Commissioner, Cuttack.

6.	*O'Malley's*, p. 34.

7.	*Surendra Sai,* p. 128.

8.	*Sambalpur*, p. 355.

9.	Letter No. 113 dated 9 February 1858 from Cap. Leigh to Cap. Dalton; Letter dt. 7 August, 1861 from Secretary to Government of Bengal to the Commissioner, Cuttack.

10.   *Veer Surendra*, p. 175.

11.   Notification dated 25 August 1858.

12.   *Surendra Sai*, p. 182.

13.   *Veer Surendra*, p. 130.

14.   Letter dated 9 October, 1858 from Lt. B.V. Ashe, Deputy Commissioner, Raipur to W.R. Forster, Deputy Commission, Sambalpur.

15.   *Veer Surendra*, p. 183.

16.   Letter No. 408 dated 24 July 1860 from Cap. Elliot, Deputy Commissioner, Raipur to Forster, Officiating Deputy Commissioner, Sambalpur; Letter No. 81 dated 8 August 1860 from Cap. C. Elliot, Deputy Commissioner, Raipur to Maj. E.K. Elliot, Commissioner, Nagpur.

17.   Letter dated 26 August 1860 from Cap. C. Elliot, Deputy Commissioner, Raipur to aj. E.K. Elliot, Commissioner, Nagpur.

18.   *Veer Suirendra*, p. 188.

19.   D.O. letter dated 19 September, 1860 Camp : Nurrah from Cockburn to C. Elliot, Deputy Commissioner, Raipur.

20.   D.O. letter dated 8 October 1860 from Forster to Elliot, Deputy Commissioner, Raipur.

21.   *Veer Suirendra*, p. 189.

22.   Letter No. 5625 dated 29 October, 1860 from H. Bell, Under Secretary to Government of Bengal to the Deputy Secretary to Government of India (Foreign Department).

23.   Letter No. 5580 dated 19 November, 1860 from Deputy Secretary to Government of India (Foreign Department) to the Secretary, Government of Bengal.

24.   Letter No. 235 dated 23 July, 1860 from H.B. Impey, Deputy Commissioner, Sambalpur to R.N. Shore, Commissioner, Cuttack.

25.   A petition in Oriya dated 8 December 1857 to Babu Brahmanand Das, Assistant to the Superintendent of Tributary Mahals.

26.   Letter No. 9 dated 4 February, 1861 from Cap. J. Smith, Principal Assistant Commissioner, Cuttack; Letter No. 14 dated 13 March 1861 from R.N. Shore, Commissioner, Cuttack to Government of Bengal.

27.   Letter No. 2125-A dated 10 August 1861 of E.H. Lucington, Secretary to Government of Bengal to Commissioner, Cuttack.

28.   *ibid.*

29.   *ibid.*

30.   Letter No. 214 dated 13 august 1861.

31.   Letter No. 235 dated 23 July 1861 from H.B. Impey to Commissioner, Cuttack.

32.   Letter No. 131 dated 16 April 1858 from Forster to Commissioner, Cuttack.

33.   Letter No. 344-A dated 11 February 1861 from Under Secretary to Government of Bengal to Commissioner, Cuttack.

34.   Letter No. 14 dated 13 March 1861 from R.N. Shore, Commissioner, Cuttack to Secretary, Government of Bengal.

35.   *Guide to Orissa Records*, IV, p. 39, Sl. No. 53.

36.   Letter dated 12 October 1860 from Officiating Deputy Commissioner of Raipur to Deputy Commissioner, Sambalpur.

37.   *Veer Surendra*, p. 199.

38.   Letter No. Nil dated 12 October 1861 of Deputy Commissioner, Raipur to Deputy Commissioner, Sambalpur.

38a.   *Liife of Surendra Sai,* p.

39.   Letter dated 12 October 1861 from Officiating Deputy Commissioner, Raipur to Deputy Commissioner, Sambalpur (Madhya Pradesh Secretariat, Judicial Department, Case File No. 4 of 1861).

40.   *ibid.*

41.   *OJR* Vol. 145, E.T. Travor to Deputy Commissioner, Sambalpur No. 11 dated 12 March 1861.

CHAPTER 5

THE TURNING POINT

Major H.B. Impey : Policy of Moderation

Major H.B. Impey took over the charge of Deputy Commissioner of Sambalpur in March 1861. He did not fail to learn from the failures of the measures of his predecessor Forster in suppressing the rebellions. He knew it well that the people were very much after restoring the Raj at Sambalpur. *Zamidnars, Garhtteas, Gauntias* – the leaders of the people – had been disaffected by land settlements. The revocation of, or imposing tax on, *muafi* grants of *Brahmottar* and *Deovattar* had disgruntled the people in general and the Brahmins and the estate holders in particular. He knew it further that military operations, which had failed to yield expected results, could not be carried on for long. Restoring peace and order had become the necessity. Bringing people into confidence was the need of the hour.

Impey knew that the rebels had a very efficient system of espionage supported by people. They could cause havoc by the time the Government would be apprised of it. The repressive measures of the Government would not be conducive in the prevailing state of things. He was convinced that army operations 'had failed in the past and must fail' because of the difficult terrain of the district and the astonishing adaptability of the rebels to jungle and mountaineering life'.

So Maj. Impey began his administration with the sincere intention of establishing peace. In fact, his period marked 'a turning point in the history of Sambalpur'. He followed a policy of conciliation with the rebels. He tried to open communication with the leaders who had marauding bands under them. He tried to keep track of two of the important bands – one under the two brothers, Hathi Singh and Kunjal Singh of Ghens *Zamindari* and the other under Khageswar Dao of Lakhanpur *Zamindari*. For that purpose, he contacted some village headmen. Impey instructed Lt. Dolmage for the reconnaissance which was kept a guarded secret. Dolmage took the help of the *Gauntia* of Bhokta on May 1861. Simultaneously a party under Lt. Cornish had come from Singhbhum under orders of the Deputy Commissioner Cap. Birch to know about the activities of the rebels in Rampur *Zamindari*. The rebels got to know about the movement of the two parties through informers and fled into Himgir jungles[1].

The rebels resorted to sporadic disturbances instead of large scale organizations. It has rightly been observed:

> If it were only a body of armed mutineers, they (the British) were fighting, they could have won the war and even crushed the enemies. If it were a concentration of troops (of rebels) fighting from a single stronghold or a number of strongholds their (the British) victory would not have been so elusive. They were not fighting against any king and his kingdom. The Britishers had to fight for these four years against the people who under the leadership of the local leaders offered resistance, which was peaceful except on rare occasions. The more enthusiastic of them turned out to be activists and always remained in the vanguard. These patriots had to face encounters often not out of choice but forced by the circumstance. It was similar to the resistance of the Spaniards against king Joseph, the brother of Napoleon who tried to enforce French regime in Spain[1a].

The failure of Dolmage's mission did not disappoint Impey. He himself decided to meet the Rajas as well as the people and win them over to his point of view. He personally met the kings of Bamra, Patna and Sarangarh and persuaded them to convince their peoples about the futility of support to the cause of rebellion. Most of the *Rajas* and *Zamindars,* however, still supported Surendra Sai. He told the people that he would try "to amend the wrong done by depriving (them of) the land grants", to their deities and "Goddess Samaleswari". He pointed out the mistakes of his predecessors who thrusted a revenue settlement without proper verification of their (people) rights and customs to the lands[2]. Impey realised that 'the public who had all through acted as a sympathetic bandwagon contributed to their (rebels) strength'. So he wrote to the Commissioner, Cuttack that in Sambalpur

> It is easier to execute than quell lawlessness because every
> one small and great, was in league with the rebels and the
> general feeling was anti-British in character[3].

Impey tried to contact Mitrabhanu, Surendra's son utilize his services to go to Surendra and Udanta who were living on the hilly region of the border of Sambalpur and Bamra. He contacted a *Gauntia* to collect information about the whereabouts of the two rebel leaders. But the *Gauntia* was detected, interrogated and let go by the men of the two brothers with a warning that he should not come on such an errand again.

Impey got to know that Udant and Mitrabhanu were separately living somewhere away from Surendra Sai, whereas Kunjel Singh and Hathi Singh were living in

Borasambar. The rebel leaders regularly visited Surendra Sai, by one or two, they were attending to him and his orders were carried out by all of them.

So it was observed that 'Surendra Sai will ever be captured but by a promise of life'. Impey wrote to the Commissioner, Cuttack

> Though Surendra Sai and his brother Udant Sai are undeserving of any mercy, policy dictates the grant of mercy to them[4].

Maj Impey realised the untold suffering and privation of the rebels. They had been living amidst jungles and hills in the vagaries of nature, starving, suffering from sickness. Some of them were rotting in Zails and were passing through agonizing days and depression of mental state. On the other hand, Government officials and army personnels were also thoroughly exhausted in the operations and actions against the insurgents. Further they were living under insecurity of life and property, in unhygienic climate and inhospitable areas during operations. People, *Zamindars, Garhtteas, Gauntias* and Government and army people thus all wanted peace and settled state. At that juncture, Impey's policy of appeasement, conciliation and pardon came as a blessing to the Tract.

The proposal of adoption of amnesty of Maj. Impey transmitted through the Commissioner of Cuttack to Government of Bengal and then to Government of India. The Government of India considered the proposal of amnesty and issued a Proclamation in October 1861. It offered:

> "amnesty and restitution of estates to those insurgents who had joined Surendra Sai and his brothers, provided they surrendered themselves within a month and a half with effect from the day of the Proclamation"[5].

It also guaranteed life to Surendra, Udant and other brothers, and 'free pardon' to Mitrabhanu in the event of their surrender within forty days from 11 October 1861.

Reactions to Impey's Policy

However, many on the sides of both the rebels and the Government personnels were against the policy of Impey. Instead of receiving the proposal in proper spirit, the rebel leaders prepared themselves for another round of rebellion. The failure to win over any leader to his side and reports of disturbances disheartened Impey. He, out of despair, wrote to the authorities, that probably his steps led to the belief:

> Resistance would eventually succeed against the British who were hesitant to establish possession in this problematic district[6].

The rebels again moved through the length and breadth of the surrounding areas of Gangpur, Khariar, Bindra-Nawagarh. The Deputy Commissioner of Raipur informed Impey of insurgent activities on the border region of Sambalpur and Raipur in the *Zamindaris* of Khariar and Bindra-Nawagarh providing support to them[7]. The execution of Kolabira *Zamindar* Karunakar Naik, despite declaration of amnesty, due to communication gap, shook the belief of the people in the intention of the Government. They thought that Government was hoodwinking them[8]. Fresh arrivals of forces at Sambalpur further increased doubts of people. Some of them again created disturbances. *Dak* communications were disturbed to some extent. However, two rebel leaders Khagga Naik and Kanha Naik surrendered before the Commander of Bengal troops, Dyer. Dyer, like Impey, was sympathetic to the people. He reported that good results might come from the conciliatory policy of Impey and so he decided to postpone military operations for a few days. It was for Dyer's intervention that 30 supporters of Karunakar Naik, *Zamindar* of Kolabira were retried and acquitted.

Despite all odds, Impey who was supported by R.N. Shore, the Commissioner of Cuttack, did not give up of hope for the success of his policy. Although he was taking a firm step to stamp out any action of insurgency, he issued instructions to all army units to exercise restraint and moderation. He was sure that after a protracted struggle in which they had fought valiantly and suffered a lot and had become totally run out the rebel leaders would come to him for establishing terms.

As regards the officials, those of Raipur and Nagpur had a sharp reaction to the policy of Impey. Cap. Lucie Smith, Deputy Commissioner of Rairpur, who was the Officer-Commanding in the successful campaign in Manikgarh hill wrote a letter to the Commissioner, Nagpur against the liberal attitude of Impey on 4 April 1861. He was against pardon to Kunjel Singh who murdered the *Zamindar* of Deori, Maharaja Sai who had rendered valuable service to the British Government against the Sonakhan *Zamindar* Narayan Singh in the critical time of 1857. He expressed his anguish as follows:

> It surely can not be the intention of Government that the man (Kunjel Singh) who was foremost in the outrage, who still retains as captive the daughter and son-in-law of the murdered man, is to go unpunished and to be restored to his estate and honours. Ghens is but a few days' journey from Deoree, and with what feelings the Deori family would watch the triumph of Koonjal Singh, in what light it be viewed by the *Zamindars* of both the districts ?[9]

Political expediency, rather than sentimental or emotional considerations for Impey was the need of the hour. So such reaction as that of Lucie Smith did not in any way influence him. On such reactions he expressed his views to Commissioner of Cuttack in a letter of 2 August 1861 elaborating that Surendra Sai:

> "descended from an notoriously troublesome Chauhan family. His uncle and father were specimens of these lawless spirits which the power of the native Chiefs was insufficient to subdue. These established right by might. Rebellion and anarchy was almost the rule of their days. If they were temporarily subdued by subsidiary agencies, such men always waited for their opportunity for revenge on the neighbours whose aid had contributed to their defeat. If a Sambalpur *Zamindar* was called upon to act against Surendra Sai, the result was that Surendra Sai and his brother ultimately avenged themselves by attacking the *Zamindar* and slaying him and his family members. It actually happened in the case of the Rampur *Zamindar.* This was so because the rebel was educated in lawlessness and the system then in vogue tended to draw out the evil elements of cruelty and self will in that wild and uncivilized dis;position"[10]

So according to Major Impey the guilt of Surendra Sai and others should not be judged by the 19th century standards of European morality.

Regarding the escape of Surendra Sai from the Hazaribagh jail which was raised in some quarters, he remarked:

> "He was released by the sepoys, strangers to him. It was natural that once again at large, finding disturbances the order of the day he should cast a venture for the recovery of an estate. Had he never rebelled, probably it would have fallen to his share as the rightful and acknowledged heir of the late Rajah Narayan Singh. The whole country invited itself to him and though the majority have deserted him, still it is perceptible enough that general sympathy is not entirely deadened"[11].

Major Impey meant business and so he put emphasis in his letter that Surendra Sai the mastermind of the disturbances could never be captured. Although he did not deserve mercy, policy dictated that it should be granted to him so that the district could be reclaimed from that state of disturbance. He further stated that some liberality shown to Mitrabhanu, the son of Surendra Sai, might influence Surendra Sai and his brothers and lead to their surrender.

Thus Major Impey in his letter to R.N. Shore, Commissioner of Cuttack urged upon him to recommend to the Government adoption of a policy of conciliation so that in pursuance of that policy general pardon be offered to the rebels and if they submitted, their confiscated estates be restored to them. Such a policy was "the best measure for restoring order in that long disturbed province"[12].

R.N. Shore appreciated the views of Major Impey and strongly recommended his letter to the Secretary to the Government of Bengal. He submitted that the Lt. Governor of Bengal might consider the guarantee of life for Suredra Sai, Udanta Sai, and Mitrabhanu Sai. He referred to the murder of the family of the *Zamindar* of Rampur, for which it was generally believed that Surendra Sai and Udanta Sai were transported for life. He observed that "due allowance must be made on account of the severe barbarous acts in which the crimes were committed. It was not a deliberate murder by a civilized man, but rather an act of wild feudal revenge". Regarding his release from the Hazxaribagh Jail, Shore also stated that he had not run away but was set free by the sepoys. Further, after that forced release they had surrendered to Capt. Leigh at Sambalpur. He further pointed out that when Surendra Sai first took resort to revolution, his first supporter was the *Zamindar* of Rampur whose family he destroyed.

"The *Zamindar,* therefore, could have no reason to complain if the murder was avenged as he proved a traitor to Surendra Sai".

R.N. Shore agreed with Impey regarding the case of Mitrabhanu and he strongly pleaded for granting pardon to Surendra Sai and his brothers. He started that he was advocating the proposal with much reluctance because he saw no other choice unless the Government were prepared to entertain an infinitely larger force to suppress the rebellion[13].

The Lieutenant Governor of Bengal after due consideration of the proposal of Major Impey and the recommendation of R.N. Shore, Commissioner of Cuttack, sanctioned the offer of a free pardon to all rebels who would surrender, excluding Surendra Sai, Udanta Sai and Mitrabhanu Sai[14].

Major Impey was glad to receive the orders of the Government regarding the guarantee of free pardon and he understood that the orders implied the restitution of the estates of those who would surrender. Accordingly he issued the proclamation on 24th September, 1861. In pursuance of that the rebels who had been convicted and were in confinement in the jails of Cuttack and Sambalpur, were all released in order to raise confidence of the people in the sincerity of the declaration of the Government.

Process of Surrender of Rebels Begins

The first to surrender in response of the Proclamation were the *Zamindars* of Rampur and Parkulunda who were not only given free pardon but were allowed to get back their confiscated estates. "It was an admirable beginning and went a long way to change the political atmosphere that was vitiated with disbelief and suspicion".

However, it brought no response from other rebel leaders and their followers. That was probably due to the exclusion of the names of Surendra Sai, Udanta Sai and Mitrabhanu Sai – the three heavy weights – from the Proclamation. So Major Impey, the Deputy Commissioner of Sambalpur with the approval of Government issued a second Proclamation on 11th October 1861 in which free pardon was offered to Mitrabhanu Sai and a guarantee of life to Surendra Sai and Udanta Sai provided they would surrender before the 20th November 1861.

Impey saw no signs of the surrender of the three and was diappointd. He knew that the only alternative was war, operation, arrests and punishments in which dase all his calculated policy would end in fiasco. He had been preparing for military operation and organizing a large force for wars with the rebels, while talking of peace to do needful after the stipulated date of the Proclamation was over. Major Impey expected arrival of large quota of the forces from Chhotanagpur[15] as well as from Nagpur and the Lt. Gvoenor of Bengal assured some help including forty elephants. A proposal of maintaining the *Beldar* fighters of Central Provinces by imposing the cost of maintenance on kings of Khariar and Bindra-Nuagarh, rebel-friendly states,was under the consideration of Government of India also.

Some of the officials pointed out the escape of Surendra Sai from Hazaribagh Zail, after which he started disturbances in Sambalpur to become king of Sambalpur, which was a criminal offence. Some others were for more vigorous military action against the rebel leaders to capture them. Still some others referred to the attack on

Rampur Zamindar in the early part of the Rebellion and destruction of some members of the family of the *Zamindar* and loot of his property.

Search of Rebels

Attempts were made to ascertain the whereabouts of Surendra Sai. The Raja of Kokair (Kankair) in Raipur district took great pains to know about the sojourns of Surendra Sai and the rebel chiefs through spies. It was ascertained that Surendra Sai was at the foot of Gurah Pahar near Sunabeda village (Khariar State) with followers. Govind Singh, son of Narayan Singh of Sonakhan *Zamindari* was staying in a village with ten followers at a distance of three *kos* from Sunabeda village. Hathi Singh and Kunjal Singh were camping at the foot of the Khorik Pani pahar five *kos* from Surendra Sai with six followers. The Officiating Deputy Commissioner, Raipur passed on the information to the Deputy Commissioner, Sambalpur requesting him to keep the matters very secret as the rebels had partisans everywhere in the country[16]. Major Impey, on his part, did not however want to act hurriedly to capture Surendra Sai though the time limit of surrender according to the Proclamation had already expired by that time.

Surrender of Rebels after Proclamation

The release of the rebels from the jails helped to create a favourable condition. Large number of rebels including *Gauntias* and *Zamindars,* who were suffering from many hazards of the jungle life and loss of kiths and kins, realised the sincerity and goodwill embodied in the Proclamation of the Government and they started surrendering with hopes of leading a better life. The important rebel *Zamindar* to surrender was Karnahar Naik of Kolabira who came back to his forfeited estate with thirty-six followers. Khagu Naik, the brother of Karnahar and Kanhai Naik, the sons of Khagu who were being considered "beyond doubt the most influential if not most powerful of he rebels" also surrendered[15]. When Major Impey intimated R.N. Shore the Commissioner of Cuttack about the surrenders of the rebel *Zamindars* and many important rebels, the latter could not believe in such statements and was rather annoyed at the liberality of the Deputy Commissioner in implementing the terms of the proclamations by restoring the forfeited estates. He expressed the opinion that Major Impey "exceeded his instructions in issuing Proclamations guaranteeing not only pardon but also restitution of properties".

Shore's Arrival at Sambalpur Expediting Conciliation

During his journey from Cuttack to Sambalpur in December 1861, an unfortunate incident had taken place at Sambalpur. Karunakar Naik, the *Zamindar* of Kolabira, who had surrendered, was executed due to communication gap. His 36 followers were released. The incident made Shore aggrieved as that would betaken taken as breach of faith on the part of the Government. He wrote to the Government of Bengal that the policy of restitution of the confiscated estates of the rebels who had surrendered in response to the Proclamations might be approved as that would restore confidence of the people in the Government which had been rudely shaken by the execution of the *Zamindar* of Kolabira. The Government of Bengal agreed with Shore and expressed "deepest regret" for the breach of faith with Karnahar Naik and ordered restoration of his properties".

Restoration of Estates

R.N. Shore praised the judicious measures of Impey regarding conciliation with the rebels and winning confidence of the people[18]. He further agreed with Impey that the estates of the rebels which had been confiscated and settled with others should be restored to the original owners in case of their surrender. This liberal policy particularly related to the estates of Kolabira, Rampur, Bheren, Paikulunda, Khariar and Kurkut.

Besides that, Impey was also prepared to make fresh grants to the rebel Chiefs on their surrender, Lok Nath Panda, the Brahmin *Gauntia* of the village of Rampella, Adhapara and Kumarbandha, who was almost to be hanged in 1857 because of his rebellious activities in support of Surendra Sai, was made the proprietor of nineteen villages assessed at half rates for a period of forty years. Mrutyunjaya Panigrahi another Brahmin supporter of Surendra Sai and a notable rebel of considerable influence, was also generously frewarded[17]. The liberal attitude of R.N. Shore and Impey removed suspicion from the minds of the rebels regarding the motive of the Government and created very favourable climate for further negotiation with others for their surrender[20]. In fact, both Shore and Impey took resort to direct communication and negotiation with the rebels with great personal risk. Very often they took the help of reliable and loyal *Gauntias* who were deputed to the rebel haunts to persuade them to surrender for a life of peace and happiness.

Surrender of Mitrabhanu

Impey's mission proved to be a success when Mitrabhanu, the only son of Surendra Sai, was persuaded to surrender on 7th January 1862. That was a fateful occasion and Impey was overwhelmed with joy and surprise, cordially greeted him and assured him of the restoration of the two *Lakhraj* villages which were being enjoyed by him before the rebellion.

Udanta on the fence

Negotiation with Udngta Sai was started but he apprehended that he was afraid to go for submission since imprisonment for life was still hanging over his head. R.N. Shore took up the case in his own hands and sent a *parwanah* to Udant Sai, persuading him to meet him without any apprehension and guaranteed him life and free pardon. He even assured him that if direct negotiation with him would fail to satisfy him, he would be free to go back without being molested. But Udanta Sai still hesitated if not refused.

Udant and Dhruv Sai's Surrender

Some loyal *Gauntias* who had acted as the emissaries, met R.N. Shore and requested him not to go for forward action and suggested an alternative measure to induce the rebels to surrender. According to them Dhruva Sai, who was then living with his brother Udanta Sai, had a large family, the members of which were almost starving for want of any means for subsistence. The destitute children of Dhruva might be prevailed upon to induce their father to submission who in his turn would be able to prevail upon Udanta Sai. R.N. Shore felt very much relieved and requested the Deputy Commissioner Impey to immediately try that measure. Dhruva Sai was persuaded by his sons to respond to the generous gestures of Major Impey. On 17 January 1862 both Udant Sai and Dhruva submitted to R.N. Shore.

The Lieutenant Governor of Bengal intimated R.N. Shore, Commissioner of Cuttack at his Sambalpur camp by telegram that free pardon had been sanctioned in favour of Udanta Sai. With that, shore was convinced that military operations would no longer be required in the district and the surrender of other rebel Chiefs was only a matter of time. He, therefore, decided that the presence of the 9th Police Battalion was no longer required in Sambalpur and accordingly, Major Rattray left Sambalpur with his mounted Police force on the 10th February.

Surrender of Hathi Singh

Udant was employed to convince Hathi Singh about the sincerity of the Government in their policy of pardon and restitution of properties. Hathi Singh was readily given pardon and the estate of Ghens was restoreded to him.

Negotiations with Surendra

N.K. Sahu has observed:

> The surrender of Mitrbhanu Sai, Udanta Sai and Dhruva Sai, as well as, of Hathi singh, Lokanath Panda, Mrutyunjaya Panigahi and other leaders of the Revolution had considerable impact on the mind of Surendra Sai. He (Surendra), however, could realize that the revolution and the consequent military action over a long period of time had done get harm to the people, many of whom had suffered inhuman torture by the British and had been killed or maimed and had also lost their near and dear ones. Villages had been burnt and depopulated, cultivation in general greatly damaged and trade and occupations considerably affected year after year, as a result of which the economic life of the district had been completely shattered.
>
> From the side of the British, Surendra Sai was made to understand that the rebellion in other parts of India had long since been suppressed and Government was in a

position to requisition huge force from all over the country to crush the resistance if he did not decide to surrender. He was told that his son Mitrabhanu "a weak young man", had been offered the Lakhraj villages in free tenure, his brother Dhruva Sai was manifesting loyalty and he would be given liberal pension for support of the large family and that was also the case with Udanta Sai who had full confidence in the sincerity of the Govoernment[21].

Surendra Sai painfully decided to close down the revolution not as a vanquished, but accepting in a dignified manner the offer of peace of the British which emanated from their inherent weakness. He knew well that the imperialists would never revive the institution of *Rajgi.*

The direct negotiation with Surendra Sai started and Impey, in order to keep the ball rolling, sent his trusted "Gomasthas" along with Udanta Sai to persuade him to come to terms. The Central provinces were constituted on 2nd November 1861 and the administration of Sambalpur was transferred to the new Province on 30th April 1862. Udanta Sai in course of discussion with Surendra Sai hinted at the point that they hoped to get better treatment from the new Central Provinces Government. Surendra Sai told them that the band of Paiks of Kamal Singh who were with him and "who had followed him and his fortunes" would not leave him unless they were paid the arrears of pay. When Impey heard of it, he could understand that the Paiks of Kamal Singh might be the barrier for the surrender of Surendra Sai, so he guaranteed the payment to the persons who advanced the money to Surendra Sai for the arrear payment[23].

Historic Meeting : Surrender of Surendra

The meeting between Surendra and Impey took place on 16th May 1862 at some place near Sambalpur town. It was then heavily raining and the impression of Impey was that Surendra Sai was then 'in rather a fidgety way'[23]. Sufrendra Sai agreed to surrender on guarantee of "life, liberty and free pardon"[24].

Surendra Sai, his staunch followers Gajraj Singh (elder brother of Kamal Singh) and his nephew Khageswar Dao, as well as, Khageswar (popularly known as Nunha Dewan) and Feteh Singh, two brothers of Janardan Gartia of Paharsirgida surrendered. Kunjal Singh, the younger brother of Hathi Singh, *Zamindar* of Ghens was then seriously ailing and he expressed his desire to surrender after recovery. Only Kamal Singh who was notable among the principal rebels remained at large and refused to surrender[25].

The facts relating to the surrender of Surendra Sai was reported to the Chief Commissioner of Central Provinces by Major Impey on 16th May 1862, the very day of that historic event and the Chief Commissioner, Central Provinces on his turn informed the Governor General in Council that Surendra Sai "the pretender to the *Gadee* of Sambalpur" had surrendered[26]. R.N. Shore also intimated the news to the Government of Bengal. Although Sambalpur had been transferred to the Central province, Shore thought that the news of surrender of "the last and chief rebel" would be received with interest and satisfaction by the Lieutenant Governor.

The Governor General in Council considered Rupees 1200 per annum "quite sufficient" for Surendra Sai and was pleased to sanction that amount as pension for him for life. It was pointed out that the Deputy Commissioner's proposal for a larger pension for Surendra Sai because of his being the Chief of the family was neutralized by the fact of his having been "the most contumacious and troublesome of the insurgents"[27]. The Governor General sanctioned an aggregate amount of Rs. 4600 for the pensions of the family of Surendra Sai and further agreed that the pensioners should take out part of the pensions in the free-hold villages to be made over to them for their lives[28].

The Governor General in Council commended the services of R.N. Shore and Major Impey for restoring tranquility in Sambalpur. He was, however, of opinion that "conciliation has been carried to its utmost limit", but "he would not regret that, if the result would prove that the permanent pacification of the district had been effected"[29].

Her Majesty's Government learnt with satisfaction that "Soorunder Sahai" had resigned all pretensions to the *Gadee* of Sambalpur and that the four years' rebellion had at length been brought to a close. Her Majesty's Government took into consideration the observation of the Officiating Commissioner of Cuttack "that from various causes there has been a very strong desire among all the influential people in the country to see the old dynasty restored and we cannot treat this feeling with contempt. We must be prepared to meet and conciliate it by placing its objects in a position both of comfort and respectability". With reference to these considerations and the position of the Chauhan family, Her Majesty's Government agreed to overlook the past conduct of the respective esta holders, the governor General in Council reserving himself the power of continuing any particular grant beyond its ordinary term, if the special circumstances of the case appeared to warrant such indulgence"[30].

Kunjel Singh and Kamal Singh

Of other notable rebel leaders, only two Kunjel Singh of Ghens and Kamal Singh of Lakhanpur did not surrender, Kamal Singh with his followers – Mahadev, Bjoy Rout, Gumaru and Hara Bagarty was still a source of headache to the British authorities. He is said to have been recruiting followers from the tribal people and creating terror for the *Zamindars* and *Gauntias* who supported the British Government. Dacoities, loots and murders were said to have been commited by his inspiration. They have been described as dacoits, *choohars*, *budmashes* in British records. Most of the dacoities were made in broad day-light but the dacoits could not be traced as they got safe hideouts in "houses common people" who were mortally afraid of them.

Kamal Singh further fanned public discontentment which took a very severe turn in 1863. He openly declared to have been fighting for the cause of Surendra Sai. Various rumours of correspondence and communication with Surendra Sai were also in the air. A reward of two thousand rupees was declared on the head of Kamal Singh. Maj. Impey himself proceeded towards Barapahar hill to capture Kamal and Salik Ram Beriha. He failed in his mission. The unhealthy climate and exertion of operation told upon his health. He fell seriously sick and died at Sambalpur in December 1863. He was captured in May 1866 while he was moving in Sarangarh State by the local Raja. He was transported to Asurgarh jail to be detained there for life[25].

Kunjel Singh and his premier associate Salik Ram Bariha were arrested in January 1865 and kept in Sambalpur jail. The Chief Commissioner of Central Provinces authorized the detention of both of them even if they would be released on appeal[26].

Despite all those ups and downs, coercion and punishment and a spirit of revenge against Surendra Sai and other rebels by the new Deputy Commissioner Cumberledge appointed on 19 January 1864 following death of Impey, and Police Superintendent Beril, people in general were still in favour of restoration of a king. They knew it that the British Government would never do it. Yet they never gave up attempts. It was revealed when a large number of eminent people presented a representation to Richard Temple, Chief Commissioner, Central Provinces during his visit to Sambalpur in March 1863. They had pointed out the inconveniences of the British system of administration in Sambalpur and that tranquility would never come to prevail unless a Chauhan ruler be seated on the throne of Sambalpur kingdom. The Chief Commissioner was astonished to receive such a petition. The spirit of revolution was still lay latent among the people, although they knew nothing would be done with regard to their demand.

Hathe Singh of Ghens who had surrendered in February1863 and was restored to Ghens *Zamidnri*, was also arrested by Cumberlege. He was sentenced to seven year' imprisonment, but later on transported to Kalapani (Andamans) where he died. Bari Singh, his brother, was confined in Sambalpur jail till his death[33].

References

1.   *Veer Surendra*, pp. 202-203.

1a.   *Surendra Sai*, p. 133.

2.   *ibid,* pp. 134-5.

3.   *OJR*, Sambalpur Records, Vol. 145 dated 3 July 1861.

4.   *ibid,* H.B. Impey to R.N. Shore, Commissioner, Cuttack No. 319 dt. 28 August 1861.

5.   *Sambalpur Papers*, Impey to R.N. Shore No. 462 dt. 9 November 1861.

6.   *ibid.*

7.   Deputy Commissioner, Raipur to Maj. Impey – B.C. Judicial 4/1861 (quoted in *Orissa in the 19th Cenutury* by Mukherjee, P.K. (p. 284).

8.   *OJR* Sambal;pur Ppers: R.N. Shore to Government of Bengal Nos. 439-440/30 December 1861.

9.   Letter dt. 4.4.1861 from Cap. Lucie Smith, Officiating De;puty Commissioner, Rai;pur to De;puty Commissioner-in-charge, Commissioner's office, Nagpur.

10.   Letter No. 319 dt. 2nd August 1861 from Maj. Impey to R.N. Shoroe.

11.   *ibid.*

12.   Letter dt. 8 June 1861 from Maj. Impey to R.N. Shore.

13.   Letter No. 259 dated 7 September 1861 from R.N. Shore to Secretary, Government of Bengal.

14.   Letter No. 2098-A dated 7 August 1861 from E.H. Lucington, Secretary to Government of Bengal to R.N. Shore, Commissioner of Cuttack.

15.   Letter dated 16 October 1861 from Maj. Impey, Deputy Commissioner of Sambalpur to Officiating Deputy Commissioner, Raipur.

16.   Letter dated 3 December 1861 from Deputy Commissioner, Raipur to Deputy Commissioner, Sambalpur.

17.   Letter dated 15 December 1861 from Maj. Impey to R.N. Shore.

18.   Letter No. 438 dated 28 December 1861 from R.N. Shore to Secretary, Government of Bengal.

19.   The recommendation of R.N. Shore for rewards in terms of both land and money to those who suffered due to support and assistance to Government was forwarded by Secretary of Government of Bengal vide his Letter No. 860 dated 31 May 1862 to Government of India. The sanction order of the Governor General in Council ws conveyed by Secretary, Government of India vide his Letter No. 371 dated 9 July 1862 to the Officiating Chief Commissioner, Central Provinces.

20.   Letter dt. 31 March 1862 from R.N. Shore, Commissioner, Cuttack to Secretary, Government of Bengal.

21. *Veer Surendra*, pp. 219-20.

22. Letter dated 25 September 1862 from Assistant Secretary to Chief Commissioner, Central Provinces to Secretary, Government of India (Foreign Department).

23. Maj. Impey's private letter dated 23 July to Mrs. C. Temple, Nagpur.

24. Letter dated 16 May 1862 from Maj. Impey to Secretary to Chief Commissioner, Central Provinces.

25. *ibid.*

26. Letter No. 60 dt. 25 May 1862 from Cap. H. MacLenzie to Col. H.M. Durand, Secretary to Government of India (Foreign Department).

27. Letter No. 590 dated 19th June 1862 from the Under Secretary to Government of India to the Chief Commissioner of Central Provinces.

28. Letter No. 657 dated 15th July 1862 from the Secretary to Government of India to the Chief Commissioner of Central Provinces.

29. Letter dated 13th November 1862 from the Secretary to the Government of India, Foreign Department, to the Secretary to the Government of Bengal.

30. Letter No. 11, Political, Dated 17the February, 1863 India Office London, from C. Wood Secretary of State to His Excellency the Right Hon. The Governor General in Council.

Her Majesty's Government considered the Services of Major Impey, the Deputy Commissioner of Sambalpur in procuring the submission of the rebels and concluding the arrangements to be entitled to Commendation.

31.   Letter No. 1273 dated 8 May 1866 from Secretary gto Chief Commissioner, Central Provinces to Secretary to Government of India (Foreign Department).

32.   Letter dated 20 January 1865 from Secretary to Chief Commissioner to Commission of Chhatisgarh Division (Case File No. 24 of 1865, Judicial Department).

33.   *Who's Who, Indian Martyrs,* III. (ed. P.N. Chopra).

CHAPTER 6

THE TURN OF TIDE: ARRESTS AND PUNISHMENTS

Sir Richard Temple, the Chief Commissioner, Central Provinces in a long minute wrote to the Secretary to the Government of India:

> The Sambalpur district was perhaps the very last district in India in which the embers of the disturbances of 1857 were finally stamped out. In 1857 a rebellion against the British authority was raised by Soorunder Sahi, a relative of the former Raja for some years in the Hazaribagh jail and escaped early in the Mutinees[1].

The Government of India considered the inconveniences with regard to maintenance of law and order during the Rebellions in the Sambalpur district (1857-62). So for effective administrative control, it was transferred from the jurisdiction of the Commissioner of Cuttack to that of Central Provinces on 30 April 1862. The primary job of the Government was to reorganize police administration to suppress lawlessness in times to come. J.N. Berill was appointed as Superintendent of Police. Somehow he came to form an opinion that Surendra Sai was the source of all troubles although the latter was living peacefully at Bargon near Sambalpur after his surrender. He tried his best, but failed to convince Maj. Impey, the Deputy Commissioner, Sambalpur about the involvement and abetement of Surendra in all disturbances. In May 1863, there were some disturbances on the southern areas (*dakshina-tira*) of the Mahanadi. One of the miscreants Malin Singh, said to be a follower of Kamal Singh, was captured by Berill. It is said that he was made to confess that:

> Surendra Sai still kept Kamal Singh and Kunjal Singh in arms in order that they may keep the *Gauntias* who were supposed to be in favour of the British rule in perpetual dread of being plundered or murdered[2].

However, Kamal Singh's marauding bands created terror by their attacks on the *Gauntias* who supported the British in present Bargarh district area. Mahadev a supporter of Kamal was killed by the *paiks* of Kodabaga *Zamindar* and Rup Singh's *Paiks* also encountered rebels in jungles of Ambabhona Police Station near Lakhanpur.

Kamal Singh is said to have declared that he was fighting for the cause of Surendra but Impey did no believe in that. On the other hand, he said that Kamal was utilizing the name of Surendra to get popular support and 'to poison the confidence of the authorities in Surendra Sai'. Various rumours regarding complicity of Surendra spread throughout the length and breadth of the district. One such was "Surendra Sai has run off" into wilderness of jungles, which people believed for sometime. But Maj. Impey remarked:

> The cry was evidently (raised) by the accomplice of Kamal Singh Dao with the hope that I would act upon it and send off to apprehend him. The promotees of the cry knew that such a course would, if Soorunder Sahi heard of it, result in his flying – becoming of fear, a rebel again, or if he had been apprehended, this district being blown into a blaze and then Kamjal Singh Dao would have gained his end"[3].

Berill, Superintendent of Police, Sambalpur tried his best to bring Surendra's name in all disturbances and pave the ground to book him. He employed one Dayanidhi Meher, a low-profile man, as spy who concocted all sorts of Stories that his intelligence could create, including one that a conspiracy was in the offing to murder all Europeans in Sambalpur for which they (the rebels) were raising a force at Jeypore etc. Maj. Impey turned down all such stories.

Major Impey, on the other hand, decided to hunt down and apprehend Kamal Singh and Salik Ram Bariha by launching an expedition himself. He wrote to Lt. Col, Balmain, the Commissioner of Chhatisgarh, to immediately send more forces and at least four camels and some elephants. But there was delay in getting response and Impey proceeded towards the Barapahar hills with an escort of sixty infantry men, dozen of sowars and a contingent of *Paiks* supplied by the Raja of Khariar with the avowed purpose of capturing Kamal Singh and Salik Ram Bariha. He failed to apprehend the rebel leaders and the operations in the unhealthy jungle region told upon his health. He fell seriously ill and died at Sambalpur in December 1863.

LAKANPOOR
DIBRUGH
PAHAR SIRIGIDA
ATTADIRA
BAMAGARH
DAGDIA
SINGORA
STRATEGY OF SURENDRA SAI
OPEN BATTLE
ZALUPDHGH
MADLABHANATA
JHARAGHAI
SALUI
SASON
KUDOSALI
SAMBALPUR
MANESWAR
DADANHU
GUNDERPUR
MUNDHLA
HUMA
DAMA

The Reversal of Impey's Policy

N.K. Sahu has observed:

> The death of Major Impey marked a drastic change of the policy and attitude of the British administrators in Sambalpur. He was the only responsible British officer to have proper understanding of the nature and behaviour of Surendra Sai and had implicit faith in him. Surendra Sai also had great regard for Impey and had genuine belief in his sincerity of purpose. The liberal policy of Major Impey succeeded because of his honesty and his understanding of the human values that were in Surendra Sai and he remained firm and steadfast in his policy and principle till his last. His death brought about a sudden change in the fate of Surendra Sai and marked sharp turn of the courses of events in the history of the revolution of Sambalpur. It gave an opportunity for the British Police and administrators to be indulged in plans and intrigues of low order to suppress the revolution of the patriots[4].

Major A.B. Cumberlege assumed charge on 19th January 1864 as the Deputy Commissioner of Sambalpur. He was determined to make a reversal of the policy of late Major Impey and finish the leaders of the revolution. On the eve of his assumption of charges, the Raipur Police surprised a band of Kamal Singh in the vicinity of Sapte *Zamindari* of Khariar. The rebels fled away leaving their personal effects. Police found there two palm leaf letters, one of which was alleged to have been written by Surendra Sai to Kamal Singh and the other by Kamal Singh to Surendra Sai. In the first letter Surendra Sai thanked Kamal Singh for sending his letter to the *Raja* of Jeypore and assured him that if the *Royats* and *Gauntias* would fail to make him *Raja*, he would join him after full moon in *Phagoon*. In the second letter Kamal Singh agreed to come down on the full moon day of the month of *Paus* to have "*moolkat*" with Surendra Sai, Dhruva Sai, Medini Sai, and Lal Baboo (Mirabhanu Sai). He would take Khageswar and

400 men with him to Bargaon. Referring to the first letter Cumbrlege declared that the discovery of the letter was quite providential and "it put the finishing stroke to prove the treason of Soorundr Sahi"[5].

Berill, the Superintendent of Police, impressed Cumberlege that "the surrender of Soorunder Sahi and his relations in May 1862 was nothing but a blind (decision) and that he (Surendra Sai) never for a moment abandoned the determination to risk everything for the *Gadee* of Sambalpur". The arguments of Berill were strengthened by the confidential reports of the spy Dayanidhi Meher who fabricated evidences regarding plan of surprise attacks by the conspirators headed by Surendra Sai. That led Cumberlege to say that the country was in 'a critical condition' and the cause of all disturbances was Surendra Sai who should have been arrested long before for restoring tranquility in Sambalpur. He remarked, "the late Major Impey was so completely blinded by Soorunder Sahi that he would not listen to Police officers like Berill and Capt. Stewart, Deputy Inspector General of Police, Central Provinces".

Major Cumberelege started brisk effort for apprehending Surendra Sai and other leading rebels. There were exchanges of letters between the Deputy Commissioner of Sambalpur and the Commissioner of Chhatisgarh and between the latter and the Chief Commissioner, Central Provinces almost everyday. The correspondences centered round the fact that Kamal Singh and his nephew Khageswar Dao were in league with Surendra Sai and his party and they were making large scale arrangement for a surprise attack on Sambalpur with a force organized at Jeypore to murder all the Europeans and to restore the native rule. The Commissioner of Chhatisgarh wrote a long letter to the Secretary to the Chief Commissioner, Central Provinces, on the 19th January 1864 soliciting the orders of the Chief Commissioner to arrest Surendra Sai and all others and to send them to Raipur for trial[6].

In the above mentioned letter the Commissioner remarked that after the return of Surendra Sai to Sambalpur "his name was used as a stalking horse by all or every vagabond till 1862" when he got amnesty which had been misplaced. There was an organized movement which convinced the authorities that the parties who were leniently dealt with were still dissatisfied and they were intriguing with the discontented Brahmins. He referred to the "grand Urjee" which was submitted to Chief Commissioner, Central Provinces Richard Temple to restore native rule and remarked "then the eyes of the authorities began to be opened to the falseness of Surendra Sai's fiction. It was then understood that all the lecturing of Udanta Sai was mere acting to mislead the Deputy Commissioner". He stated about Kamal Singh and his followers who were in open rebellion and pointed out that although many of his followers were either apprehended or killed he was still in active rebellion, murdering, robbing and burning in villages in the name of Surendra Sai. Of late Kamal Singh became unaccountably silent and it gave rise to grave suspicion. It might be a lull before a storm.

The Commissioner also referred to the spy Dayanidhi Meher who furnished information to the Police that a plot had long been in existence for murdering Major Impey and other Europeans and "coercing the British Government directly or indirectly by keeping up constant irritation in the district into restoring the native rule". In that connection he drew the attention of the Chief Commissioner to the meeting of the weaver, in his own house, with Khageswar Dao "the bravo of the malcontents" at which Major Impey, Capt. Stewart and the Inspector Mohan Singh were present and Khageswar told the spy that there would be an outbreak of rebellion for which armed men were being recruited in Jeypore and that he would be the first man to murder Major Impey. The silence or inactivity of Kamal Singh might be a prelude to the storm.

Cumberlege further pointed out that every thing was not right and the time was very critical. The Police were foreigners and not being acquainted with the local language could not mingle with the people and collect information. The Tahsildars who were local men were unreliable as they were either sympathizers of the rebels or were influenced by them out of fear. The *Garjat* Chiefs desired to appease the rebels not only due to fear but also due to the fact that they were after getting rid of the British rule. The Raja of Sonepur assisted the *Khand* rebellion of Baud in 1862, "the Raja of Sarangarh showed signs of wavering, and the Rajas of Patna, Khariar and Bindra Nuagarh were already under a cloud". The Commissioner furnished a dozen of corroborative evidences to prove that Surendra Sai was plotting against the Government.

The Chief Commissioner in his turn made various comments and queries on the several points in the reference of the Commissioner, Chhatiisgarh and gave definite instruction on the line of action to be taken against Surendra Sai and others. The Chief Commissioner could not readily believe that any of the *Garjat* Chiefs had complicity in any sedition or conspiracy against 'the constituted authority'. That had not been proved by the Commissioner although he had taken months together to collect the information.

The Rajas were more or less neutral, if not loyal. They conducted themselves in their own ways. As regards the people of Sambalpur, he was of the opinion that there was not a general ferment and disloyalty and political disaffection could not be shared by the general public. If there was sufficient evidence to take legal action against Surendra Sai and others, he replied that the Commissioner had already been in possession of instructions demi-officially conveyed to him. The Chief Commissioner did not desire to force a charge of treason on Surendra Sai and his adherents, if the desired effect could be otherwise gained. If, however, they were unwilling to go outside and commit any overtact of treason, then the legal process was to be resorted to. He pointed out that he had already expressed this view in his letter No. C dated the 22nd January, 1964 to the Government of India. The Chief Commissioner said that he would rely in the Commissioner's making a judicious use of his discretion thus entrusted to him.

As regards the supply of more force to Sambalpur in the event of deportation of Surendra Sai and others after arrest, the Chief commissoner said that the he (Deputy Commissioner, Sambalpur) could summon them from Raipur, if circumstance so warranted it[7].

The Commissioner replied to the queries made by the Chief Commissioner regarding his views about the Garjat Chiefs. He declared that each of the Rajas was under the impression that Surendra Sai would somehow achieve his position as the Raja of Sambalpur with the concomitant feudal superiority over them and so great was their dread of his tool Kamal Singh that there was a sort of tacit understanding between

Surendra and the *Rajas* .They (the *Rajas*) were to remain neutral so that their possession would be subjected to as little annoyance as possible from the gangs of the outlaws who, in great degree, depended upon them for supplies. He stated that the mention had been made at best in one, if not in more of the treasonable correspondences of the complicity of the 18 *Gurjats* under Sambalpur. Those letters have been forwarded to the Chief Commissioner direct.

The Chief Commissioner still believed that the *Garjat* chiefs were free from complicity of Surendra Sai's rebellion and accordingly he wrote to the Secretary to Governor-General in Council[8]. The Government of India called for information regarding the Tahasildars.

The correspondences of the Deputy Commissioner of Sambalpur indicate that the rebels were ready with the plan of an attack on Sambalpur which was imminent. On his part, he was ready to counteract. He waited for Mitrabhanu Sai, who had returned at 4 P.M. on the 22 January 1864 from Chhotanagpur, to be arrested with his father. The arrests were made most efficiently in the night of 23 January, which invited the attention of the authorities to the good services rendered by the Europeans[9]. A detailed report was submitted by the Chief Commissioner to the Government of India justifying the action of the local authorities. He commended the services of the officers for the appreciation of His Excellency the Governor-General. He requested His Excellency to write to the Government of Madras with regard to the Jeypur Raja as that *Zamindari* was under the Vizagpatam Disitrict[10].

The Deputy Commissioner at once gave a finishing touch to the plan of arrest of the rebel leaders in consultation with Cap. Stewart, the Deputy Inspector-General of Police in securing simultaneously all of those whose cases had been previously determined, viz. Surendra Sai, his son Mitrabhanu Sai, his brother Udanta Sai, Dhruba Sai, Medini Sai, Harihar Sai, Aglu and Brajmohan - sons of Dhruba Sai, Chaitan Sai, Murdhan and Gurgar Sai, sons of Dhruba Sai, Robagee, Lokanath Gartea and Dharani Misra - friends and counselors of Surendra Sai, Khageswar Dao, Murali Dao and Mohan Dao- three brothers.

Lt. Col. J.G. Balmain, Commissioner, Chattisgarh, who made a number of allegations, noted above, against Surendra Sai, Khageswar Dao and others, was so much enthusiastic about arrest of the rebel leaders that he personally came down to Sambalpur to supervise the arrangements for execution of the plan of the Deputy Commissioner, Sambalpur. It was decided that all the persons would be apprehended by surprise attacks simultaneously. If any of them would get slightest indication about what was going to take place, they would run away and the revolution might recur and the whole country would be in a deluge. So the district authorities kept everything about the plan top secret and did not intimate "to any sepoy or policeman to be in readiness until the moment came to strike".

The details of the plans for apprehending all these persons were finalized on 23 January 1864. On that day at about sunset, Cumberlege got it approved by the Commissioner Balmain who was present at Samblpur[11].

The Police party proceeded towards Bargaon in that very night from Sambalpur and arrested Surendra, his son Mitrabhanu, Dharanidhar Mishra, Loknath Panda, Mundha – a nephew of Surendra and an illegitimate son of Dhruv Sai. Thereafter some of them left for Talab village and arrested Udant Sai and Medini Sai. Then they proceeded to Tabla village and arrested Dhruv Sai and his son Braj Mohan. Berill and Cumberlege rushed to village Bonda and arrested Khageswar and his brothers in a surprise attack. Thus, by daybreak of 24th January things as planned were over. Jagabandhu Hota, Padmanabh Guru, Mrityunjay Panigrahi, Sradhakar Mallik were arrested on 26 January, 1864.

The officiating Chief Commissioner had already sanctioned deportation for trial at Raipur the following fifteen prisoners – Surendra Sai, his three brothers, his son, four sons of Dhruva Sai, Khageswar Dao and his two brothers, Lokanath Panda, Dharanidhar Misra and Sradhakar Mallick. On the 26 January 1864 those prisoners were transported to Raipur under the escort of a Company constituting a Police guard of 20 sowars and 20 foot police commanded by Lt. Rideout.

The following was the descriptive roll of State prisoners transported from Sambalpur to Raipur on 26 January 1864. The names of three sons of Dhruva Sai did not find place in the lis[12].

Name of the Prisoner	Father's name	Age	Village	Place of residence	Caste	Profess-ion
Soorunder Sahi	Dhurm Singh	55	Bargam	Sambalpur	Chhatri Chouhan	Govt. prisoner
Oodunt Sahi	-do-	53	Talub	-do-	-do-	-do-
Droob Sahi	-do-	45	Tabla	-do-	-do-	-do-

Mehdunee Sahi	-do-	22	-do-	-do-	-do-	-do-
Gurjun Rai (Sahi)	-do-	18	-do-	-do-	-do-	-do-
Khugeswar Dao	Besumboer	40	Banda	-do-	Gond Gauntia	-do-
Minakuthun Dao	-do-	25	-do-	-do-	Gond cultivator	-do-
Mohun Dao	-do-	26	-do-	-do-	-do-	-do-
Mitrabhan Sahi	Soorundar Sahi	20	Khinda	-do-	Chhatri Chauhan	-do-
Lokanath	Gungdhur Baban Panda	55	Rampally	-do-	Brahmin	-do-
Dhurnee Misr	Bharatee Misr	34	Khinda	-do-	-do-	-do-
Siridakur	Juthee	25	Pyhebat	-do-	Rajput	-do-

Subsequently, Jagabandhu Hota, Padmanabha Guru[12a] and Mrutunjaya Panigrahi were apprehended and deported to Raipur for trial. The Commissioner decided that those against whom sufficient evidence could not be adduced, "would be deported as a political measure"[13].

Kamal Singh, Kunjal Singh and Salik Ram Bariha remained at large without being apprehended and they continued to be the source of anxiety for the British officers. Cumberlege sent Lt. Bawie to the Ghens *Zamindri* to arrest Kunjal Singh, but the attempt proved futile. Lt. Berill gathered information that Kunjal Singh was regularly coming to the village Barmal near Ghens to spend the night there and he used to go back to the jungle early in the morning. So in order to catch hold of him before dawn it was decided to make a surprise attack on the village Barmal and Bawie. Berill started in the night of 7 March 1864 with a band of cavalry men and rode a distance of sixty miles to reach the Ghens *Zamindari.* But they were misled and lost the way. By the time they reached Barmal it was broad day-light and Kunjal Singh had already escaped. The Chief Commissioner further directed that Cumberlege, the Deputy Commissioner, Sambalpur, should be instructed not to misuse his discretionary power in his zeal and desire to punish the offenders. While investigating the cases he should not entertain the views which might appear violent and partial and should consider the charges in calm and judicious frame of mind[14].

Cumberlege was determined to book both Hathi Singh and Bairi Singh of Ghens *Zamindari* and got them arrested on charges of treason . The main charge against Hathi Singh was that he harboured his rebel brother Kunjal Singh in his *Zamindari*, thus filling "his cup of uniquity to the brim"[15]. Hathi Singh was tried and was sentenced to 7 years' transportation on that charge[16]. Subsequently early in January 1865, Kunjal Singh and Salik Ram Bariha were captured and the Chief Commissioner authorized the detention of Kunjal Singh "if he be acquitted of charges brought against him" and regarding Salik Ram Bariha he also directed that he was to be detained "should he be released on appeal"[17]. Both Kunjal Singh and Salik Ram Bariha were confined to the Sambalpur jail.

The British Administrators were not satisfied with the punishment meted out to these patriots and further plans were made for wreaking cruel vengeance on them. Charges of murder and arson were brought against Kunjal Singh and Salik Ram Bariha and both of them were executed after a mock trial, while Hathi Singh was transported to Andaman where he breathed his last[19]. Bairi Singh, the brother of Hathi Singh, was confined to Sambalpur jail till his death.

Kamal Singh remained to be apprehended and a reward of Rupees two thousand had been declared on his head[20]. He was captured at the beginning of May 1866 when he was roaming in Sarangarh in the guise of a Fakir[21]. The Raja of Sarangarh had been recently given the status of a feudatory Chief and out of his zeal to exhibit his loyalty he betrayed Kamal Singh, the outstanding patriot and leader of the Revolution, and handed him over to his British overlord.

Trial of Cases

The Deputy Commissioner, Raipur was entrusted with enquiry based on witnesses and incriminating materials and he framed charges against the accused person of (i) preparation to wage war against the Queen between December 1862 and January 1864 and previously thereto under Sec. 122/109 of IPC (ii) a betting preparation to wage war against the Queen under section 100 and 123 of IPC, (iii) concealing design to wage war against the Queen. After a trial for about 4 months in the Court of Sessions Judge Lt. Col. J.G, Balmain, who was the Commissioner of Chhatisgarh also at that time, judgment was made on 23 June 1864.

Surendra Sai, Udant Sai and Khageswar Dao found guilty of the first charge and vide Sec. 122 of IPC were sentenced to transportation of life with forfeiture of all their properties.

Dhruv Sai, Medini Sai, Loknath Panda, Mrityunjaya Panigirahi, Jagabandhu Hota and Sraddhakar Mallik were found guilty of second and third charges and were sentenced to same punishments.

Mitrabhanu, Mohan Dao, Dharanidhar Mishra and Padmanabh Guru were sentenced to transportation for seven years each on the basis of the third charge.

The accused filed a petition of appeal in the Court of the Judicial Commissioner, John Scalet Campbell. He found the judgment of the lower court as 'confused and wanting in point' and its proceedings as 'very far from being clear and satisfactory, the documents of evidence as 'gross forgeries' prepared subsequent to arrest 'to bolster up a case which was palpably weak'. So the Judicial Commissioner reversed the judgment of the Sessions Court by acquitting all the prisoners of the offences charged against them on 18 August 1864. They were all released, but Surendra Sai and his three brothers Udant, Druv and Medini, his son Mitrabhanu, Khageswar Dao and Loknath Panda – those seven were detained by the executive order of the Chief Commissioner, Central Provinces vide Regulation III of 1818[22]. The Governor-General–in-Council approved the detention[23].

Thereafter the Commissioner, Chhatisgarh recommended the deportation of all the detainees to a distant place for peace and security reasons of people of Sambalpur[24]. The Chief Commissioner, Central Provinces recommended the names of seven persons to Governor General-in-Council for 'reasons of State and the security of the British Dominion from internal commotion[25]. They were Surendra, his son Mitrabhanu, his brothers Udant, Dhruv and Medini, Khageswar Dao and Loknath Panda.

The Governor-General agreed as proposed by the Chief Commissioner, Central Provinces and passed order that they should be confined at Nagpur[26]. Finally on the proposal of I.G. Police, Central Provinces, they were transported to the fortress of Asirgarh (East Nimar District of Central Provinces) on 8 June 1865.

Thus the Rebellion of the Sambalpur Tract came to an end.

References

1. Letter dated 23 January 1865 from Secretary to Chief Commissioner, Central Provinces to Secretary to Government of India.

2. Letter No. 35 dated 24.2.1864 from Maj. Cumberlege, Deputy Commissioner, Sambalpur to Commissioner, Chhatisgarh.

3. Letter No. 1 (Sambalpur Disturbances) dated 12 November 1863 from Maj. Impey, Deputy Commissioner, Sambalpur to Commissioner, Chhatisgarh.

4. *Veer Surendra*, p. 247.

5. Letter dated 24 February 1864 from Cumberlege to Commissioner, Chhatisgarh.

6. Letter No. 38 dated 19 january 1864 from Commissioner, Chhatisgarh to Chief Commissioner of Central provinces.

7. Letter No. 477 dt. 27.1.1864 from Secretary to Chief Commissioner, Central Provinces to Commissioner, Chhatisgarh (National Archives).

8. Letter No. 820 datd the 20th February, 1864 from Capt. Hector Macburn, Secretary to Chief Commissiobner to Colonel H.H. Durand C.P. Secetary, Govt. of India, Foreign Department (National Archives).

9. Letter No. 217 dated Camp: Sambalpur, the 26th January, 1864 from the Commissioner, Chhatisgarh to the Secregary to Chief Commissioner (National Archives).

10.   From Captain Hector Mackenzie, Secretary to the Chief Commissioner to Col. H.M. Durand, C.B., Secretary to Govoernment of India, Foreign Department Letter No. 183 dated 3.2.1864 (National Archives).

11.   Commisioner, Chhatisgarh in his Letter No. 217 dated 26 January 1864 Camp: Sambalpur to Secretary to Chief Commissioner narrated arrests.

12.   *Life of Surendfra Sai*, Appendix-Q, p. 189.

12a. Padmanabh Guru was arrested by the Raja of Sone;pur and the Commissionr of Chhatisgarh conveyd his satisfaction for the loyal service of the Raja. See letter No. 254 dated 8th February 1864 from the Commissioner of Chhatisgarh to the Deputy Commissioner, Sambalpur.

13.   Letter No. 254 dated 1st February 1864 from the Commisioner of Chhatisgarh to the Deputy Commissioner, Sambalpur. See also the letter of the Commissioner to the Deputy Commissioner, Sambalpur, dated 11th February 1864.

14.   Letter No. 1938 dated 21 April 1864 and 2850 dated 22 June 1864 from the Secretary to the Chief Commissioner, Central Provinces, to the Commissioner of Chhatisgarh Division.

15.   Letter No. 557 dated 12th March 1864 from Cumberlege to Commissioner of Chhatisgarh. *History of Freedom Movement in Orissa*, Vol. II, p. 53 foot note 163.

16.   Letter dated 21.9.1984 from Cumberlege to Commissioner, Chhatisgarh.

17. Letter dated 20 January 1865 from Secretary to Chief Commissioner to Commissioner, Chhatisgarh (Case File No. 24 of 1865, Judicial Depaprtment).

18. *History of Freedom Movement of Orissa*, Vol II, p. 71 foot notoe 204.

19. *Who's Who Indian Martyres*, Vol. I, Kunjal Singh.

20. Cumberlege's letter dated 20 May 1871 to Secretary to Chief Commissioner (also foot note 18 above)

21. Information obtained ffrom letter No. 1273 dated 8 May 1866 from Secretary to Chief Commissioner, Central Provinces to Secretary to Government of India (Foreign Depargtment).

22. Letter dated 23 January 1865 from Secretary to Chief Commissioner, Central Provinces to Secretary to Government of India (Foreign Depargtment).

23. Letter dated 23 January and 17 April 1865 from Secretary to Government of India to Secretary to Chief Commissioner, Central Provinces.

24. Letter No. 3161 dated 8 September 1864 from Commissioner, Chhatisgarh to Secretary to Chief Commissioner, Central Provinces.

25. Letter No. 4533 dated 19 September 1864 from Secretary to Chief Commissioner, Central Provinces to Secretary to Government of India (Foreign Department).

26. Letter No. 252 dated 3 November 1864, Fort William from Col. H.M. Durand to Secretary, Chief Commissioner, Central Provinces.

CHAPTER 7

MOVERS AND SHAKERS
OF
THE REBELLION

It is difficult to make profiles of the hundreds of rebels who have suffered and, even those small who have sacrificed themselves at the gallows or by the fire or in the prisons. What to speak of the activities of the common rebels, even the names of the principal leaders have remained obscure till very late. *The Freedom Struggle of India* by Bipan Chandra (National Book Trust, New Delhi) and, surprisingly *Who's Who of Indian Martyrs*, Vol. III edited by P.N. Chopra (Department of Culture, Ministry of Education, New Delhi, 1973) have not mentioned all their names. The contributions and sacrifices of the entire male members of a few of the *Zamindar* families, and some individual leaders as well, were legendary and, as such, they deserve special mention in the annals of the Freedom Struggle of India.

Of all the *Zaminari* families, those of Khinda, Ghens, Lakhanpur and Kolabira etc. deserve special mention in the pages of the annals of the Freedom Struggle for their bravery, suffering and sacrifices.

KHINDA

Balaram Sai and six (out of seven) of his nephews (sons of his brother Dharam Singh) viz, Soonder or Surendra, Udant, Dhruv, Ujjal, Chhabil, Medeni are famousfor their heroic acts and sufferings. They kept the fire of rebellion against the British Government burning from 1827 till 1862.

Balaram Sai

He was a scion of the *Zamindar* family of Khinda. He was the guardian and guide of all of his nephews following the death of their father. He supported the claim of his eldest nephew Surendra for the throne of Sambalpur kingdom following the death of the king Maharaja Sai in 1827. The widow queen Mohan Kumari made an offer of the office of *Dewan* to him but he gave up the office to support the claim of Surendra.

The death of the Lakhanpur *Zamindar* Balabhadra Dao in the encounters with the army of the king of Sambalpur made Balaram take revenge on Rampur *Zamindar* Dariar (Durjay Singh) who gave information about the whereabouts and meeting of Balabhadra with Balaram and Surendra at Debrigarh. The members of his family except the *Zamindar* and one of his sons, were killed by his nephews Surendra and Udant.

In 1840, while proceeding to Patna State, Balaram and his nephews Surendra and Udant were attacked by an army of the king of Sambalpur Narayan Singh at Deheripali near Sambalpur town and arrested the three. Lt. Col. J.R. Ousley, Agent to Governor-General, South-West Frontier Agency who was on a visit to Sambalpur at that time, tried the case of the murder of Rampur *Zamindar* and sentenced Balaram to life imprisonment while Surendra and Udant were sentenced to imprisonment of five and seven years respectively. They were sent to Hazaribagh Zail where Balalram died.

Surendra Sai

The most powerful of the rebel leaders came to limelight as a claimant to the throne of Sambalpur when the king of Sambalpur Maharaja Sai died, without a heir in 1827. He was the eldest of the seven sons of Dharam Singh of Khinda, a *muafi* estate of Sambalpur kingdom. He was born on the full moon day of *Pausa* corresponding to 23 January 1809. Surendra and his brothers were brought up under the loving care of his uncle Balaram. He taught them three R'S and trained in handling arms and weapons of the time, physical culture and jungle warfare. Surendra, particularly among the brothers, proved to be more successful. He was an excellent horseman. From his very childhood, he developed a strong feeling of patriotism and heroism which had profound effect on his guardian, guide and uncle Balaram. It was for Surendra's rebellion that he gave up the Dewanship of Sambalpur kingdom. His brothers were also very much devoted to him and inspired by his ideals of heroism and patriotism. His only son Mitrabhanu, born on 1839, in the midst of the early phase of the rebellion of his father also came under the revolutionary zeal of his father and members of family. N.K. Sahu has beautifully put it as:

> The physical character of Khinda and its neighbourhood
> having thick forests covered with tall sal trees, the frowning
> Maula-Bhanja hills, the swift flowing Ib river and the
> sparkling brooks, the bears and leopards, chittals and
> sambars, as well as, the sturdy aboriginals – everything

around conspired to fill the imagination of Surendra Sai with
heroic and patriotic ideas (*Veer Surendra Sai*, p. 78).

After his claim to the *Rajgi* of Sambalpur was set aside by the British who installed on the *gadi* Narayan Singh of Barpali in 1833, Surendra started revolution vigorously. The revolution was suppressed by the king with the help of the British. He was arrested with his brother Udant and uncle Balarm at Deheripali (Sambalpur), while they were going to Patna for collecting men, money and arms, by a sudden attack and sent to Hazaribag Zail in 1840.

After Surendra was set free from the Zail by the mutinied Sepoys in 1857, he came to Sambalpur and organized the revolution which has become popular as *Ulgulan* or The Disturbance. His brothers, son, many of the *Zamindars, Garhtteas, Gauntias* and people came out in support of Surendra.. The Disturbance continued unabated, through ups and downs till he surrendered to the British in May 1862 on a guarantee of life, liberty and free pardon by Deputy Commissioner of Sambalpur Maj. H.B. Impey.

Hardly Surendra had settled for two years, he was arrested by the new Deputy Commissioner of Sambalpur Maj. Cumberlege who was bent upon the arrest of Surendra and others who had surrendered. Surendra, his son Mitrabhanu, brothers Udant and Dhruv, Dhruv's four sons, Dharanidhar Mishra, Loknath Panda, Shraddhakar Mallik, Khageswar Dao etc. were arrested on 23 January 1864. They were forwarded to the Court of the Commissioner, Chhatisgarh after allegations were framed by Deputy Commissioner Cumberlege on the basis of some conversations between Surendra/his associates with a low-profile spy Dayanidhi Meher appointed by the British and some spurious palm-leaf letters supposed to have been written by Surendra and Kamal Singh.

The Commissioner of Chhatisgarh Lt. Col. J.C. Bolmain made a number of allegations against Surendra and others on the basis of evidences supplied by Deputy Commissioner, Sambalpur. The Chief Commissioner, Central provinces did not believe in all the evidences. He did not like 'to force a charge of treason on them if the desired result could otherwise be obtained'.

However, Balmain was so enthusiastic to arrest Surendra and others that he himself came to Sambalpur to implement the plan. It was delayed due to absence of Surendra's son Mitrabhanu who was at Chhotnagpur. He came to Bargaon in the afternoon of 22 January 1864, where Surendra was staying. The Deputy Commissioner, Deputy Inspector General of Police Cap. Stewart and Superintendent of Police, Berill secretly finalized the list of men to be captured, the time and other modi operandi on 23 January and got the approval of the Commissioner instantly. The Police party started for Bargaon about 20 km from Sambalpur at 10.30 P.M. on the same day and surprised Surendra, Mitriabhanu and others by their capture.

After the arrest the Deputy Commissioner, Sambalpur made out a strong case for their (Surendra and others) involvement in matters to revive the *Raj* and outbreak of open rebellion as well as connection with dacoities. He pleaded for their removal to Raipur for restoration of order in Sambalpur and inspiring confidence among people. The Chief Commissioner had approved the deportation to Raipur for trial. The Deputy Commissioner, Sambalpur was directed by Deputy Commissioner, Raipur to prepare a compendium of the case. Twenty witnesses and more than that number of palm-leaf documents were cited for the purpose for examination by Deputy Commissioner,

Raipur. The case was tried by Commissioner of Chhatisgarh J.G. Balmain as the Sessions Judge. Surendra and two others were found guilty of 'preparing to wage war against the Queen' under Section 122/109 of IPC and sentenced to transportation for life with forfeiture of all their properties on 23 June 1864. The accused made an appeal in the Court of Judicial Commissioner, J.S. Campbell who found the judgment to be 'confused and wanting in point'. He acquitted them of the offences charged against them on 18 August 1864.

However, the prisoners were detained by an executive order of the Chief Commissioner of Central Provinces vide Regulation III of 1818 for 'reasons of State and the security of the British Dominion from internal commotion'. It was decided to keep them confined at Nagpur. However, Inspector General of Police and Chief Commissioner, Central Provinces submitted a proposal of confining them in the Asirgarh fort (Nimar district, Central Provinces). Surendra and six others were removed to that fort from 8 June 1865. Their petition of appeal to Governor-General in Council against illegal detention in 1866 was rejected for fear of disturbances in Sambalpur district. In 1871, the question of release was raised, which fell through because of the objections of Chief Commissioner of Chhatisgarh.

After suffering from confinement for twenty years, he breathed his last at 1 A.M. on 28 February 1884.

In befitting manners, Cultural Associations of Sambalpur like *Odisha Sanskritik Samaj* and *Veer Surendra Sai Bi-Centenary Birth Anniversary Celebration Committee* etc. have celebrated the Bi-Centenary Birth Anniversary, organized meetings, set up statues and brought out Souvenirs on the occasion in January 2009.

Udant Sai

Udant Sai was the first younger brother of Surendra. He had been with his elder brother through thick and thin from the beginning to the end of the rebellion. Among others, he was with Surendra when the latter attacked the *Zamindar* of Rampur Dariar Singh who managed to escape but lost his father and son in 1840. While going to Patna State with Surendra and uncle Balaram, all the three were arrested by a surprise attack of the British and kept in Sambalpur jail. He was sent to Hazaribag zail when sentenced to life-term confinement. After 17 years, he and Surendra were set free by the Sepoys in 1857 Mutiny. He returned to Sambalpur with Surendra. But without losing time, he left for his home place, village Khinda near Sambalpur, to organize recruits for a rebel army and support among people. His organizational power was extraordinary.

During the operations of the rebels against the British army, Udant was given the charge of the Jharghati Pass, 20 kms to the north of Sambalpur on the Sambalpur-Ranchi road. He constructed an impenetrable fortress like stonework. Major Bates destroyed that by heavy firing and killed a large number of rebels. The pass fell into the British hands. Udant however managed to escape. Thereafter he took an active part in the Rebellion till his surrender to the Deputy Commissioner Maj Impey on 17 January 1862. However, the new Deputy Commissioner Cumberledge got him arrested on 24 January 1864 in his house at Talab. He was tried at the Sessions Court at Raipur and sentenced to transportation for life with forfeiture of all his properties. Although he was acquitted on appeal by the Judicial Commissioner, he was detained under Regulation III of 1818. He was confined with other rebels in Asirgarh fort where he died sometime after the death of his brother Surendra (28 February 1884).

Dhruv Sai

The second younger brother of Surendra was also a great rebel who took active part in the 1857 Rebellion under his elder brother's leadership. He with his brother Udant had surrendered on 17 January 1862. Like Udant, he was arrested and tried at Raipur in January 1864 and punished with transportation for life and forfeiture of properties and confinement in Asirgarh jail. He was, however, released on 1 January 1877 on the arrangement of fulfilment of the conditions laid down by Chief Commissioner, Central Provinces (Letter No. 4386/dated 22 November 1876 from J.W. Neill, Officiating Secretary to Chief Commissioner, Central Provinces to Commissioner, Chhatisgarh).

Ujjal Sai

The third younger brother of Surendra Sai came to light when he was organizing the tribal *Kondh* people in Patna State to support the rebellion of Sambalpur. Raja Hiravajradhar Dev knew about it and pretended to have arrested Ujjal when the Government of Sambalpur asked to do so. But when the king was asked to hand over the 'notorious rebel' he declared that he had escaped. The king was, therefore, fined Rs. 1,000 by the Cuttack Commissioner Cockburn. Later on when the king was pressurized, he betrayed Ujjal to Cap. Forster, the Officiating Deputy Commissioner, Sambalpur. Ujjal was hanged on 1 June 1858 by orders of Forster.

Chhabil Sai

The fourth younger brother of Surendra came to limelight when he was shot dead in an encounter with the British forces under Cap. Wood at Kudopali on 30 December 1857. He actively took part in the rebellion till his death. He has been regarded as a great martyr by the people till now.

Medini Sai

The sixth and youngest of the brothers of Surendra joined his brothers in the Rebellion of 1857. He was arrested in the house of Udant Sai at Talab in January 1864. Like his brothers – Surendra, Udant and Dhruv, he was also sentenced to life-term imprisonment and forfeiture of properties and sent to Asirgah fort jail where he died in 1876.

Mitrabhanu Sai

The only son of Surendra Sai, he was born in 1839. He married Krishnapriya Devi, the daughter of the Raja of Banai, but joined his father and uncles and took active role in the Revolution. He surrendered on 7th January 1862 and the Lakhraj village of Khinda was restored to him. He was, however, arrested with his father at Bargaon in the night of 23 January 1864 and was tried in the Sessions Court by Lt. Col. J.G. Balmain who sentenced him to seven years imprisonment. The orders were reversed by the Judicial Commissioner, but he was detained along with his father and others under Regulation-III of 1818 and was kept in confinement in Asirgarh hill fort. He was released with his uncle Dhruva Sai on 1 January 1877 and was brought to Banai where he resided for long thirty years. He was allowed to come to his village home Khinda in 1907. As he had no issue he adopted a boy named Giridhari from the family of Rajpur *Zamindar* in 1922 and died in October 1926 at the age of 87.

GHENS

Like the Khinda *Zamindar* family, the Ghens *Zamindar* family's contributions, sufferings and sacrifices to 1857 Rebellion in Sambalpur Tract has become proverbial. *Zamindar* Madho (Madhav) Singh belonged to the Binjhal tribe. He and his sons Hatte (Hathi), Kunjal, Bairi, Kunjal's son-in-law Govind Singh and his father Narayan Singh of Sonakhan *Zamindari* (Chhatisgarh) have left behind immortal legacies of patriotism and sacrifice.

Madho Singh

A scholar has remarked about Madho to the extent:

> Even the uncontestable leader Veer Surendra of the *Ulgulan* of Sambalpur can not be compared with Madho Singh. Madho Singh has occupied a special place in the unwritten history of freedom struggle of the peoples of the world. (*Souvenir, Jatiya Veer Surnedra Sai's Bi-Centenary Birth Anniversary,* Odisha Sanskritik Samaj, Sambalpur, 2009, p. 113).

Another scholar has remarked on the sacrifices of Madho Singh

> The sacrifices of the Ghens *Zamindar* family reminds (us) of those of Rana Pratap Singh of Mewar

(quoted in, ibid,p.114)

B.S. Guha has rightly said:

> Madho Singh died with his entire family members by supporting the legitimate claim of the uncontestable leader, the scion and heir of the Chauhan royal family of the Confederacy of the *Athara-Garhjats*. He has never fought for the fulfilment of his selfish interests.

(quoted, *ibid*, pp. 114-15)

It is unfortunate that the name of such a personage has not been found in the hundreds of books written by historians of India as well as Odisha till very late.

Madho Singh was a farmer who cultivated lands in 20 villages of Ghens *Zamindari* by himself and his sons. It was a hinterland of Sambalpur British district. He was living happily with members of his family with the income from the fields. No information is available about his education which must have been elementary if at all it was available. It is astonishing if such one could know about the risings of the tribal, the downtrodden and the affected in other parts of India and then organize the tribal people of West Odisha for the Rebellion of 1857 in Sambalpur Tract. With members of his family and relations he jumped into the fray of rebellion against a mighty power like the British.

The early phase of the Rebellion in Sambalpur which started with Mohan Kumari, the widow-queen of Maharaja Sai, as the ruler in 1827, brought Madho Singh to action. He supported the claim of Surendra Sai. Surendra had complete faith in his loyalty and support. He made him (Madho) the sentinel of the famous Singhora Pass near Sohela on Sambalpur-Nagpur road. The British forces despatched from Nagpur and Raipur were devastated by the guerilla warriors of Madho Singh. The heroism of Madho Singh was raised in discussion in the House of Lords of Britain (*ibid*, p. 117).

On 29 December 1857 the detachment of irregular cavalry under Cap. Wood was opposed at Singhora Pass. The detachment managed to outflank the troops of Madho Singh and reached Sambalpur. The Pass was captured by Cap. Shakespear in early part of February 1858. The location of the pass was very strategic. So when Shakespear left for Raipur, it was reoccupied by the rebels.

In December 1858, Cap. Forster, Deputy Commissioner, Sambalpur made a surprise attack on the fort of Ghens and captured Madho Singh. He was hanged at Sambalpur on 31 December 1857.

Hathe Singh

He was the eldest son of Madho Singh[1], the *Zamindar* of Ghens. In 1857 he played important role in strengthening the defence of Ghens and cooperated with his father in controlling communication through the Singhora pass. In February 1858 when Capt. Shakespear invaded Singhora *ghaty* with a squadron of Cavalry and opened heavy firing, Hathi Singh bravely faced the attack. A big piece of stone cracked by the cannon balls hit him at the chest and he fell unconscious. He was removed to a secret cave for treatment and the British occupied the strategic pass. But soon after that the Singhora *ghaty* was recaptured by Surendra Sai with the troops of Ghens. Hathi Singh and his brothers Kunjal Singh and Bairi Singh were a great source of strength for Surendra Sai. They were ready to sacrifice anything for Surendra. After the surrender

---

[1] N.K. Sahu (*Veer Surendra Sai*, p.337) has describd Hathi, Khunjel, Bairi as gthe grandsons of Madho Singh while other scholars consider them as sons (*Souvenir*, Odisha Sanskritik Samaj, pp. 113,115, 119).

of Udanta Sai and Dhruva Sai, Hathi Singh surrendered in February 1862 and the estate of Ghen was restored to him. But he was arrested in 1864 by Cumberlege, the Deputy Commissioner, Sambalpur, on the charge of harbouring his brother Kunjal Singh in his estate. He was sentenced to seven years' imprisonment and later on, transported to Andamans where he died.

Kunjel Singh

He was the second son of Madho Singh. He assisted his father and elder brother in guarding the Singhora Pass. He was a very loyal and trusted follower of Surendra Sai. He encamped in the Sunabeda plateau of Khariar estate. On 16th July 1860 Kunjal Singh with his son-in-law Govind Singh attacked the house of Maharaja Sai the *Zamindar* of Deoree just at noon and murdered him in cold blood as he was an active agent and supporter of the British. The Commissioner of Nagpur declared rewards of five hundred and two hundred fifty rupees for the capture of Govind Singh and Kunjal Singh respectively. When Surendra Sai surrendered in May 1862, Kunjal Singh did not surrender as he was then seriously ailing. Capt. Lucie Smith the Deputy Commissioner of Raipur strongly objected against grant of amnesty to Kunjal Singh, but the Government of India on recommendation of the Lieutenant Governor of Bengal offered amnesty to him. Kunjal Singh, however, decided not to surrender and joining hands with Kamal Singh continued the revolution. He was captured early in January 1865 along with Salik Ram Bariha and was confined to Sambalpur Jail, where he was subsequently executed on charges of murder and arson.

Bairi Singh

He was the third son of *Zamindar* Madho Singh of Ghens. He came to prominence during the attack against Bijepur *Zamindar* Gopinath Garhtia who annexed village Bhatibahal of Ghens *Zamindar* by fraud through the agency of the British officials of Sambalpur in the reign of Mohan Kumari (1827-33). He, like his father and brother Hathi and Kunjel, was an avowed enemy of the British government. He accompanied his brothers to receive Surendra Sai who was coming to Sambalpur from Hazaribag in 1857.

In 1858, when Hathi Singh was severely wounded by a piece of stone on his chest in an encounter with Cap. Shakespear at Singhora pass, Bairi was also with him. It is said that an imposter named Kenkeni brought a head of a dead soldier of Hathi Singh and presented it to the British as the head of Hathi, who was of course alive, to receive an award of five villages. Later on, the villages were taken away from him when it was proved to be false. Bairi became extremely angry with Kenkeni, killed him and hanged his head in a branch of a tree of a village which was now known as 'Kenmundi' after the name of Kenkeni (*Souvenir*, Odisha Sanskrutik Samaj, Jan 2009, p. 209).

The Singhora Pass, which was lost to the British, was reoccupied by the rebels after the departure of Cap. Shakespear after a few days . Again, the pass was placed under the command of Kunjel and Bairi, while Hathi Singh was recovering from his wound.

Bairi Singh surrendered when Hathi did so in February 1862 and, when the latter was restored to Ghens *Zamindari* the former stayed there. However, both the brothers were arrested. Bairi Singh died in Sambalpur jail.

LAKHANPUR

Balabhadra Singh Deo

He was the *Zamindar* of Lakhanpur situated about 48 kms on the north-east of Bargarh. He was an avowed enemy of the autocratic rule of the British Government and the puppet Government of Rani Mohan Kumari of Sambalpur kingdom. Thus he became a staunch supporter of the claim of Surendra Sai to the throne of Sambalpur. He got the support of the tribal people like *Gond, Binjhal* and *Chuhan* etc. of his *Zamindri* as well as the *Zamindari* of Pahadsirgida, Bheden, Kanekbira, Kolabira, Kudabaga, Loida, Loisingh, Patkulunda, Machida, Phuljhar, Raigarh and Sarangarh etc. which were either collateral branches of his family or relations. He organized them against the British. He arranged their training in guerrilla warfare and such weapons as bow and arrow, javelins, swords battle-axe etc. Debrigarh, the most strategic of the rebel fortresses during 1857 Rebellion, on the top point of the Barpahad hill was in his *Zamindari*. He got a strong stonework built at Debrigarh for garrisoning the rebels and the sojourn of principal rebel leaders like Surendra Sai. In fact, 400 to 500 rebels could be accommodated on the plains of Debrigarh, besides a cave known as *Barbakhra* which could provide shelter in rains and winter.

On 8 January 1831, Balabhadra met the British forces in a front-to-front war. *Subehdar* Gurudayal Tiwiari and *Jamadar* Gangadhar Mishra led troops of Ramgarh Battalion under the command of Cap. Wilkinson. Balabhadra burnt the camps.

Balabhadra's rebellion became fiercer after Narayan Singh became the ruler of Sambalpur kingdom in 1833. He organized rebellion under his direct supervision from Debrigarh. The king and the British Government found it difficult to curb the tide of rebellion which was growing day by day.

While Balabhadra and Surendra were at parleys at Debribgarh in November 1837, the combined forces of the British, the Sambalpur king and of the *Zamindars* of Rampur, Phuljhar and Barpali *gheraoed* Debrigarh. Surendra Sai managed to escape but Balabhdra Dao was killed in the encounter. He was one of the pioneer-rebels or torch-bearers of Sambalpur rebellion who paved the way of struggle for his sons and grandsons.

Kamal Singh

Balabhadra's eldest son – Kamal Singh[2] and another son Khageswar Singh Dao jumped into the fray of the Rebellion. The Rajput *Zamindar* of Rampur who helped the king of Sambalpur in the attack against his father and Surendra Sai was taken to task, his house was burnt and some members of his family were killed. The action endeared Surendra to the tribal *Zamindars* who came out in support of his claim to the Sambalpur throne. However, the arrest and confinement of Surendra in Hazaribag Zail thereinafter from 1840-57 by the British Government at the connivance of the Sambalpur king Naryan Singh tuned the rising flame into smoke for a long period. It apparently cooled down in the absence of Surendra from Sambalpur. In the meantime Lakhanpur *Zamindari* had been confiscated by Narayan Singh at the instigation of the British.

After Surendra's escape from the jail, Kamal Singh described as "the most faithful and powerful supporter of Surendra Sai" joined the Rebellion under Surendra's leadership. Of the five strategic hill posts, the most important one Debrigarh was under the charge of Kamal and Khageswar. They defended it from the British onslaught through numerous difficulties.

Kamal Singh was instrumental in taking revenge against Tikait Singh, a member of the younger branch of Lakhanpur *Zamindar's* family, who played treachery against the *Zamindar* family to make himself the *Zamindar.* Tikait Singh was killed. His son Jai Singh Dao approached Maj. Impey, the Deputy Commissioner of Sambalpur for the purpose of obtaining the *Zamindari,* but the latter refused as he expected rebel-

[2] Adopted from the Principal Investigator's article: "1857 Rebellion of the Sambalpur Tract : Role of Surendra Sai's Three Associates of Lakhanpur Zamindar Family" (*Souvenir,* Odisha Sanskrutik Samaj, Sambalpur, 2009, pp. 152-55).

members of Lakhanpur *Zamindari* might be lured to submission with the prospect of obtaining it.

In the later phase of the Rebellion (1858-62), Kamal Singh remained with Surendra in the Manikgarh hill of the Jonk river valley of Nawapara district (Orissa) and helped him in the military operations against the British. He was capable of reoccupying Debrigarh, the most important hill-top post of the Barapahar hill in 1861 operating from Manikgarh area.

During the time of submission of Surendra Sai, Gajraj and Khageswar and others submitted but Kamal refused to do so. The Chief Commissioner Central Provinces has been informed by Maj. Impey that Kamal was 'notable among the principal rebels remained at large'.

Kamal Singh gathered around him all discontented elements against the British. Kunjel Singh of Ghens, Mohan Singh of Sohela and his friend Salek Ram Bariha, Mahadev, Hara Bagarty, Gumaru etc. He made recruits from various tribes like *Gond, Binjhal, Kondh, Soura*. He made depredations to different *Zamindaris* suspected of anti-Rebellion stance. Broad day-light robberies were committed during August 1862 to September 1863 in which his followers were said to have been involved as known from the reports of Maj. Impey. Kamal's mission was to restore Chauhana kingship in Sambalpur and he was ready to go to any length for this purpose.

When Richard Temple, Chief Commissioner, Central Provinces, was presented a petition during his visit to Sambalpur in March 1863, duly signed by a large number of influential persons, he was surprised. He expressed his inability to restore Chauhana

Kingship and refused the representation. The popular discontent which came in its trail was utilized by Kamal. He vigorously organized the Rebellion and made raids and depredations and killed a few men. Of course, he lost his associates Mahadev and Bijay Rout during the turmoil.

Kamal's raids continued unabated. In May 1863, he made attacks on some of the villages on the southern bank (Dakhin-tir) of the Mahanadi. A few villages were burnt down by the followers of Kamal Singh. A letter on palm-leaf supposed to have been written by Kamal to Surendra was retrieved from a man by Police Superintendent of Sambalpur J.N. Berill which revealed that Kamal was maintaining liaison with Surendra Sai "in order that they may keep the *Gauntias* who were supposed to be in favour of the British rule in perpetual dread of being plundered or murdered". Berill further extorted a confession from Malin Singh, a follower of Kamal, in that regard. Major Impey, ascertained the fact from Surendra and learnt that he had no complicity in the matter.

Even when Kamal openly declared that he was fighting for the cause of Surendra, Impey believed that he was making use of Surendra's name to gather popular support. A rumour that Kamal and Surendra were planning to organize a big rising for murdering the Europeans in the district was found to be baseless.

A few days ago Major Cumberledge took over charge of Deputy Commissioner of Sambalpur after death of Major Impey, on January 1864, i.e., in December 1863 a few followers of Kamal Singh were surprised by Raipur Police at Ghooraghum in Khariar area. Two letters on palm leaves – one from Surendra to Kamal and the other from

Kamal to Surendra were found from the baggage left behind by the rebels when they ran away. Whereas Surendra thanked Kamal for sending his letter to the Raja of Jeypore, that of Kamal contained his consent to join Surendra for an informal discussion. The Superintendent of Police, Sambalpur tried to convince the Deputy Commissioner Cumberledge that Kamal Singh and his nephew Khageswar were in touch with the principal rebel Surendra and they were making a massive arrangement for a surprise attack on Sambalpur. The Deputy Commissioner was convinced of the fact that there were enough evidences about the liaison of Surendra Sai with Kamal and their followers were involved in the numerous *decoity* cases of the district. The letters were deposed in the court of Raipur.

Kamal Singh was the last known rebel to have been captured. It is said that while he was roaming in disguise as a mendicant in Sarangarh, he was captured in May 1865 by the Raja of Sarangarh who had been elevated to the status of a Feudatory Chief a little while ago. It was the expression of his zeal to show loyalty to the British Government. His action was, of course, commended and, the reward of a sum of two thousand rupees declared for the capture was paid to the Raja. Kamal Singh was sent to the Asirgarh fort jail where Surendra and 6 others had already been confined. When the question of release of the seven prisoners in Asirgarh fort came up, following their filing a petition to Governor General-in–Council in 1866, Sir Richard Temple, Chief Commissioner of Central Provinces gave the opinion that their release would be detrimental to the tranquility of the district of Sambalpur. The Governor General Sir John Lawrence, however, was not satisfied with it. Again in 1869, when his views was sought by Lord Mayo, the Governor-General, he told that they were the last batch of rebels in the 1857-58 Mutiny and were "offenders of a very incorrigible type". He apprehended that they might indulge in rebellious activities if freed from confinement. Accordingly, Lord Mayo dismissed the prayer of the petition. With regard to Kamal and Khageswar, his remark was that they were 'trusted captains' of Surendra Sai and were of 'notorious' and 'blood-thirsty' character.

In the meantime, Lokanath Panda died in the prison of Asirgarh in March 1875. Medini Sai died sometime in 1876. Again the question of release was raised in 1876 by Cap. Bawie, Deputy Commissioner, Sambalpur after smooth conduct of land revenue settlement and prevalence of law and order in Sambalpur district. The Commissioner of Chhatisgarh agreed with the proposal of releasing Dhruva Sai and Mitrabhanu Sai on certain conditions.

Ultimately Surendra Sai, Kamal Singh and Khageswar Singh remained in the jail till the end of their lives. Whereas a date of passing away of Surendra i.e., February 28, 2884 was mentioned in a medical certificate, those of the other two were not ascertained till date.

The valiant hero Kamal Singh died after languishing for an unknown period. The sufferings he might have undergone, the tortures he might passed through has remained obscure. Bravery, loyalty to leadership and the saga of suffering he has left behind will ever be cherished by a grateful posterity. Of the principal rebels, he was the one who carried on his fighting against the British for the longest period. He was one of the rebels whose contribution to bring Sambalpur Tract, a tribal hinterland of the country, into the mainstream study of 1857 Rebellion is, in deed, significant.

Khageswar Singh Dao

He was another son of Balabhadra Singh Dao, the *Zamindar* of Lakhanpur and the brother of Kamal Singh. He was a man of courage and strong will and very frank and straightforward in his dealings. He was a very trusted and loyal supporter of Surendra Sai and was a veteran warrior. He was with his brothers Kamal and Nilambar in the supervision of the most important and centrally located Debrigarh fort on the Barapahar hill.

Maj. Impey, Deputy Commissioner, Sambalpur learnt that Khageswar was alone leading a group of rebel-fighters while Hathi and Kunjel Singh of Ghens were leading another. After Udant's submission he was sent to Khageswar for the latter's submission. He surrendered in May 1862 along with Surendra Sai, but the estate of Lakhanpur was not restored to him which was considered to be a violation of the terms of proclamation of Major Impey according to which it should go to Kamal, the legitimate *Zamindar*. Khageswar Dao was, however, allowed to stay in the Bonda village near Lakhanpur as the *de facto* owner of that small estate. Although he surrendered, he had strong feeling of support for his heroic brother Kamal Singh who continued the revolution. Khageswar along with his brothers was arrested in his house at Bonda in the morning of 24 January 1864 and was tried in the Sessions Court by Lt. ol. J.G. Balmain. He was sentenced to transportation for life with forfeiture of all his properties, but later on was set free by the Chief Judicial Commissioner. He was, however, detained under Regulation-III of 1818 and taken to Asirgarh for jail when he spent the rest part of life till death.

Nilambar Singh

Balabhadra Dao'son and Kamal Singh' younger brother. He joined in 1857 Rebellion with his elder brother. He was in charge of the defence of Debrigarh fortress of the Barapahar hill with his brothers Kamal and Khageswar. He wanted to take revenge of the death of his father against the British. He organized guerrilla fighting in many places. In one November night of 1862 he entered into Sambalpur town with a group of rebel-fighters and killed two soldiers of the British forces and wounded eight of them (*Souvenir*, Odisha Sanskrutik Samaj, p. 126).

When Cap. Wood and Cap. Woodbridge were proceeding to Singhora, en route Barapahar they were attacked there with gun-shots by Kamal Singh and Nilambar. They also made the boulders bound with creepers roll down on the enemy soldiers and created panic and destruction.

Kunjel Singh of Ghens, Kamal Singh and Nilambar Singh of Lakhanpur did not surrender even after Surendra and his brothers' surrender. They kept the rebellion alive for sometime more from the hideout of Debrigarh. Several attempts of Maj. Impey to capture the two brothers were of no avail. It is said that Cumberlege got Nilambar arrested after arrest of Surendra Sai and others in 1864. However, the account of the rest of his life is not available to us.

Mohan Singh Dao

Another brother of Khageswar Singh Dao. He was arrested with his brother from his house at Bonda in the morning of 124 January 1864 and was tried in the Sessions Court by Lt. Col. J.G. Balmain who sentenced him to imprisonment for seven years. But the Judicial Commissioner reversed the orders of the Sessions Court and he was set free and allowed to reside in the Bonda village.

KOLABIRA

Karunakar Naik

He was *Zamindar* of Kolabira, one of the principal rebel leaders, like Madho Singh of Ghens and Balabhadra Dao of Lakhanpur. He was a collaborator of Surendra Sai from 1827 to 1861 when the latter launched a rebellion, for obtaining *Rajgi* of Sambalpur, against the British. He belonged to the *Gond* tribe and, as such received the support of all *Gond gauntias* as well as the people of his *Zamindari.* His nine brothers, nephew Kanhei and son Krishna Chandra, Patrapali's Brahmin *Gauntia* Balabhadra Dash and *Gond sardar* Gopal Dherua of village Dulki of Jharsuguda *Zamindari* etc. were among his principal followers.

Kolabira, which was considered as a stronghold of Rebellion of 1857, was attacked in November 1857 by Lt. Hadow with MNI and forces of Cuttack. They passed through Katarbaga and Samsingha and reached at Kolabira on 6 November 1857. The British were hopeful of capture of Surendra and Karunakar but they could not get any trace of them. The villagers left the village and ran away into jungles. The British forces destroyed some houses and looted. The *Zamindar's* house was destroyed by shooting.

Karunakar's only son Krishna Chandra became a martyr in the Kudo;pali battle (*Souvenir*, Odisha Sanskrutik Samaj, p. 87) in which Chhabil Sai, Surendra's brother was killed. The son's death broke him. He thought it better to surrencder to the British and be restored to his *Zamindari* when Maj. Impey's Proclamation of Amnesty had been in vogue since 24 September 1861. He surrendered with thirty-six of his followers including his brothers who were considered by Maj. Impey "beyond doubt most influential, if not most powerful of the rebels".[3] Lt. Robinson, who was in charge of Command in the absence of Maj. Bates, did not know the terms of amnesty granted to them by Commissioner of Cuttack, tried them in the military court. Kkarunakar was sentenced to execution. He was hanged at Sambalpur on 22 December 1861.

PAHADSIRGIDA

Janardan Singh Garhtia

He was another powerful and efficient leader of 1857 Rebellion of Sambalpur. As a *Gond Zamindar* he commanded loyalty and respect from the *Gonds* and *Binjhals* of his *Zamindari* as well as other *Zamindaris* like Lakhanpur, Kolabira, Kudabaga, Machida etc. where collateral members of his family held estates. He encouraged and inspired his cousin brothers Kamal and Khageswar of Lakhanpur for the Rebellion.

Janardan fortified and garrisoned the Pahadsirgida pass.[4] It was attacked by Cap. Woodbridge on 12 February 1858. The *Gond* rebels of the *Zamindari* charged the enemy with vollies of missiles and killed a large number of British Sepoys. Except a

---

[3] Impey's Letter to Commissioner of Cuttack on 25 December 1861.

[4] Description of the fortification of the pass is available from the report of Ensign Warlow, who invaded the pass on 14 February 1858, with a map enclosed, vide Letter No. 1 dated 15 February, 1858 to Cap. Michoills from his camp Pahadsirgida.

few, the entire detachment of the Ramgarh Battalion was destroyed. Cap. Woodbridge was said to have been killed by the *Zamindar*.

The rebels' victory at Pahadsirgida on 14 February 1858 "restored the fallen prestige of the rebels and encouraged them to fight further battles with the British". In the late part of the month, however, Cap. Nicholes achieved some successes against the rebels, but with heavy loss. He managed to reach the fortress of Debrigarh and cleared it off the rebels. His two brothers Khageswar Singh (popularly known as *Nunha Dewan*) and Fateh Singh who were all along there with him surrendered to the British authorities when Surendra, Khageswar Dao and Gajraj of Lakhanpur did so on 16 May 1862.

Nunha Diwan

Khageswar Singh, a brother of Janardan Singh, was popularly known as Nunha Dewan. He joined the revolution of Surendra Sai with his brother the *Zamindar* and another named Fateh Singh. The three brothers distinguished themselves for their courage and heroism. He surrendered with Fateh Singh in May 1862.

BHEDEN (BASAIKELA)

The *Zamindar* family of Bheden like those of Ghens, Lakhanpur, Kolabira and Pahadsirgida, had played its role against the British from 1827 to 1857.

Abdhut Singh

Abdhut Singh, the *Gond Zaminar* of Bheden revolted against the installation of the Maharaja Sai's widow queen Mohan Kumari on the throne of Sambalpur kingdom. He came to light for his rebellion against the queen. His *Zamindari* was confiscated.

He was supported by a number of tribal *Zamindars* and *Gauntias* in the rebellion. The *Gond* people refused payment of revenue to Government. He looted the state godown on 23 July 1830 and created disturbances. The combined army of the queen under Banamali Rai and of the British under Wilkinson waged a war against the *Zamindar*. After fierce fighting, his supporters surrendered with weapons and, he ran away for Debrigarh. He was hotly pursued by the sepoys of Ramgarh Battalion but the rebel forces of Debrigarh resisted them with firing.

Abdhut joined in the Rebellion started by Balabhadra Dao, *Zamindar* of Lakhanpur and the combined forces were engaged in severe encounters against the sepoys of Ramgarh Battalion. The rebel forces set fire to a part of village where the British forces had pitched tents.

The rebellion spread to various parts of present Bargarh district. The *Zamindr* of Jharsuguda Govind Singh, Medini Beriha of Kharmunda and Trilochan Beriha of Pahadsirgida had joined in the rebellion in the mean time.

Cap. Wilkinson did not want to take stern measures, rather he wanted to suppress the rebellion by peaceful measures and discussion. Accordingly, he restored Abdhut Singh, Trilochan Rai, Balabhadra Rai, Sivnath Rai to *Zamidnars* of Bheden, Gad-Loisingh, Pahadsirgida, Bamanda and Kudabaga-Barepali respectively.

Manohar Singh

He was the son and successor of Abdhut. He was inspired by the ideals of his father and supported the rebellion, '*Ulgulan*' of Surendra Sai in 1857. Towards the close of 1858. Col. Forster, Deputy Commissioner, Sambalpur made a surprise attack on

Baseikela and set fire to the village. Manohar Singh gave a tough encounter and died fighting in it.

KHARSAL

Dial Sardar

Dial Sardar, the *Zamindar* of Kharsal played his role in the Rebellion of Surendra Sai in 1857. He was arrested and brought to Sambalpur where he was hanged on 3 March 1858 by orders of Cockburn, the Commissioner of Cuttack.

SOHELA (Bargarh district)

Mohan Singh

Zamindar of Sohela, he was a noted revolutionist because of which his estate was confiscated. He acted as the *Jamadar* of Surendra Sai and surrendered with Surendra Sai in May 1862. But Major Impey, in violation of the term of his proclamation, did not restore his estate of Sohela to him. So he withdrew his surrender and joined in the rebellion of Kamal Singh. He was a friend of Salik Ram Bariha and Kunjal Singh. He was an adept in guerilla fighting. Nothing is known about him after the capture of Kunjal Singh and Salik Ram Bariha.

(II) GAUNTIAS

Besides the *Zamindars,* some village headmen (*gauntias)* also played significant role in the 1857 Rebellion in Sambalpur tract.

Loknath Panda (Gartia)

He was the Brahmin *Gauntia* of the villages – Rampella, Adhapara and Kumrbandha and was a great supporter of Surendra Sai. He was a notable rebel and was almost to be hanged in 1857 because of his rebellious activities. He surrendered in 1862 and was treated with due honour by Major Impey who generously made him proprietor of nineteen villages assessed on half rates for a period of forty years. He was arrested in the morning of 24 January 1864 and tried in the Sessions Court at Raipur by Lt. Col. J.G. Balmain, who sentenced him to transportation for life with forfeiture of all his properties. But he was acquitted of all charges by J.S. Campbell, the Judicial Commissioner. Later on, he was detained under Regulation-III of 1818 along with Surendra Sai in Asirgarh fort jail where he died sometime before 1871.

Madhu Gauntia

He was the *Gauntia* (village head) of Jujomura in Loising *Zamindari* and took active part in the rebellion of 1857. He was patrolling the Badpati pass on the Sambalpur-Cuttack road with a strong band of followers in order to cut off all communications between Cuttack and Sambalpur. As the British troops in Sambalpur were falling sick in large number, two European Doctors from Ganjam – Dr. Moore and Dr. Hanson, were deputed to Sambalpur for their treatment. The European Doctors proceeded from Cuttack escorted by a detachment of sepoys and reached Rairakhol in the evening of 16 November 1857. Early the next morning while going through the Badpati pass they were attacked by the rebels. Dr. Moore was killed and Dr. Hanson managed to escape with great difficulty. The Raja or Rairakhol Bishan Chandra betrayed Madhu *Gauntia* and three of his followers, who were suspected to be responsible for the murder of Dr. Moore. They were hanged by orders of Cockburn, the Commissioner of Cuttack.

Mrutyunjaya Panigirahi

He was a great supporter of Surendra Sai and a notable rebel of considerable influence. He was the proprietor of the village Arda which was confiscated because of his rebellious activities. He surrendered in 1862 and Major Impey treated him generously and restored Arda village to him. He was arrested in 1864 from his Arda residence and was tried in the Sessions Court by J.G. Balmain who sentenced him to transportation for life and forfeiture of the properties. But J.S. Campbell, the Judicial Commissioner acquitted him of all charges and passed orders for his release.

(III) OTHERS

Padmanabha Guru

He was an inhabitant of Sonepur. (According to Pt. Swapneswar Das he belonged to the Guru family of Sambalpur). He was a supporter of Surendra Sai and was acting as his adviser. Major Cumberlege, the Deputy Commissioner of Sambalpur, requested Raja Niladri Singh of Sonepur to arrest him and the Raja carried out the request and arrested Padmanabha Guru on 8 February 1864, although he was then leaving Sonepur State and was eight miles away from Sonepur town. He was tried in the Sessions Court at Raipur by Lt. Col. Balmain and was sentenced to seven years' Imprisonment, but was acquitted by orders of the Judicial Commissioner J.S. Campbell.

Salik Ram Bariha

His role in the revolution came to light after the surrender of Surendra Sai. He strongly supported Kamal Singh who refused to surrender and continued the revolution. Salik Ram was a friend of Kunjal Singh and he operated from Patna kingdom where he got shelter and carried on depredation in the British territory. Hira Bajradhardeva the Raja of Patna connived at his activities for which he was strongly warned by the British authorities. Salik Ram Bariha was subsequently captured with Kunjal Singh in January 1865 and both the heroes were executed in Sambalpur on charges of murder and arson.

Sraddhakar Mallick

He was from Sambalpur town and was a close friend of Surendra Sai. He was arrested in the morning of 24 January 1864 in the house of a relative and was tried in the Session Court at Raipur by Lt. Col. J.G. Balmain and was sentenced to transportation for life and forfeiture of properties but was acquitted by the Judicial Commissioner.

Dharanidhar Mishra
&
Jagabandhu Hota

They were close friends and supporters of Surendra Sai. They were arrested with Surendra Sai. Dharanidhar and Jagabandhu were sentenced to 7 years and transportation for life respectively by Sessions Court, Raipur. They were set free by Judicial Commissioner J.S. Campbell later.

CHAPTER 8

CONCLUSION

The investigation has been a humble attempt to highlight a comparatively obscure aspect i.e., the role of Zamindaris, which counted sixteen on the eve of 1857 Mutiny, of the Sambalpur Tract (Orissa) in the Rebellion during 1857-62. In fact, the 1857 Rebellion, which continued vigoursly for more than five years whereas it was suppressed elsewhere in the country in a year or two, has remained sidetracked from the mainstream study on 1857 Mutiny of the country, although it was 'an integral part of the All-India Revolution of 1857-58 the objective of which was to achieve freedom from the British yoke'.

A unique feature of the Rebellion in Sambalpur Tract was that *Zamindars*, most of whom were tribals – either *Gond* or *Binjhal* – led the Rebellion both in their estates and contributed significantly to centralized leadership of Surendra Sai – a legitimate claimant of Khinda *Zamindar* family to the throne of Sambalpur kingdom, whose claim has been set aside by installation of puppet rulers by the British Government twice in 1827 and 1833. The *Zamindars* not only participated themselves but also pooled the military resources of their people majority of whom were tribal – *Gonds, Binjhals, Sauras* etc. It is noteworthy that many estate-holders – *Zamindars* and the like – *Garhtteas, Muafidars* (commonly designated as *Zamindar*) and village headmen called

Gauntia, Thekadar, Bhogra-Bhogi etc. also jumped into the fray of the Rebellion with their people. Cutting across the lines of caste or status, a number of *Brahmin Gauntias* and Caste Hindus also joined the Rebellion. Thus it became a popular rebellion against British paramountcy by the people of Sambalpur Tract. The participation was for a long time, from as early 1827, and wholehearted and, paved the way for the prolongation of the Rebellion for five years (1857-62).

Another notable feature is that the *Zamindars* and people – majority of them were illiterates, far from the civilization, lived in Sambalpur Tract which remained a hinterland of the country amidst hills, jungles and rivers. Such a land and such people, it was interesting of course, participated wholeheartedly in the Rebellion and, left behind the sagas of their patriotism, courage, heroism and sufferings which have, indeed, a few parallels in the country.

To cite a few instances of Khinda, Ghens and Lakhanpur etc. in the context, all most all members of the *Zamindar* families made supreme sacrifices and ultimately perished in the fire of the Rebellion. Of the Khinda *Zamindar* family, Balaram had died in Hazaribag jail before 1857, Surendra Sai suffered imprisonment for 37 years, played the leading role from 1827-40 and again from 1857-62 and died in confinement, his brother Udant who played a vital role with Surendra also died after remaining in confinement for more than 20 years, another brother Ujjal Sai was hanged, another brother Dhruv Sai suffered imprisonment for about 13 years, another brother Chhabil Sai was shot dead and the youngest of them Medini Sai died in jail after suffering from imprisonment for about 12 years. Surendra's only son Mitrabhanu was in jail for 13 years. One can imagine the plight and privation they and their family members might have passed through.

Likewise the sacrifices of the members of Ghens *Zamindar* family have become both exemplary and legendary. The *Zamindar,* Madho Singh was hanged, his eldest son Hatte Singh was transported to Andaman, another son Kunjal Singh was hanged, third son Bairi Singh died in jail – after playing significant parts in the drama of patriotism.

In the case of Lakhanpur *Zamindari,* its *Zamindar* Balabhadra Singh Dao was killed in an encounter with the army of Narayan Singh – the puppet king of the British in 1837, his eldest son Kamal Singh who carried on the Rebellion till 1866 died in Asirgarh fort jail, grandson Khageswar, called 'the bravo of malcontents' also died in the same jail after exhibiting rare feats of bravery and patriotism.

Besides those, a number of other *Zamindars, Gauntias, Garhtteas and Gauntias* had made sacrifices of one, two or more members of their houses. A large number of other people, either individually or collectively, have also laid their lives for the cause of patriotism.

It is really unfortunate that all their names have remained in the limbo of oblivion for about a century, i.e, till 1958 when a published monograph in Oriya by Svapneswar Dash first brought Surendra Sai – the unparalleled hero and a few of his colleagues who stood as bulwarks against British autocracy to lime light. It was followed by another in English by his son A. Dash, a retired I.A.S. officer, *Life of Surendra Sai* in 1963. The name of Hatte Singh, the only rebel who was transported to Andaman came to be known, after the enquiry of Prime Minister Mrs. Indira Gandhi during her Andman visit, when it was published in *Who's Who of Indian Martyrs*, Volume III by Department of Culture, Ministry of Education, Government of India in 1973.

The Sources of the dissertation constituted mostly archival materials – letter, reports and other documents on the basis of which three books and a few articles of some research content have been written by now. The two books – *Veer Surendra Sai* (Bhubaneswar 1985) and *Surendra Sai, Pioneer of a Complete Revolution (1857)* (Sambalpur, 2002) have almost utilized the same sources on which *Life of Surendra Sai* (1963) has been written. No fresh light thus has been shed or fresh information furnished by the two. However, the present investigator has the opportunity of availing new materials, including some vernacular compositions, which came to light as a result of painstaking search of some scholars in the last three decades and, particularly, in the yesteryear when the Bi-centenary Birth celebration of Surendra Sai was celebrated throughout the length and breadth of Sambalpur Tract. Many Souvenirs, Journals and Magazines highlighting many hitherto unknown information came to light. For the first time, folksongs which have been collected from various places of the Tract have been dispassionately analyzed and utilized as a source to throw light on some obscure facts or replenish the information revealed from dependable written sources. The write-ups or articles published in the Bi-centenary magazines are of inestimable use. The investigator taking clues from the contributors went on fact finding missions and gathered some amount of source materials.

In the organization of the present Report, the role of historical geography, i.e., the physical features of the Tract, which are of course peculiar to the terrain, their bearing on, and contribution to the continuance of the rebellion has been assessed. The hills and their passes, the jungles and the environs of the river valleys have not only provided shelter and defence but determined the battle strategy of the rebels. It would have been difficult to fight against the mighty British Power with traditional weapons without the unique background of geographic features and landscape.

Thus far the developments leading to the Rebellion in the Tract have been approached from political angle. The socio-economic factors based on, or centering land system, which contributed significantly have not been given due importance. It may be said that without the intervention of the British administration in the *muafi, brahmottar* and *devottar* type revenue-free land grants and depriving the grantees of the customary privileges and rights and the people of their bread and butter − it is doubtful if the mass participation would have come voluntarily and the rebellion sustained for a long period. Due consideration has been given to Land Settlements preceding the Rebellion.

With regard to the development of political circumstances leading to the Rebellion also, the role of some of the *Zamindars* like that of Bheden, Jharsuguda and Ghens − which have not been given due importance till date − a succinct discussion has been furnished. Those rebellions were, in fact, pioneering, which paved the way for 1857's developments.

The early phase of the Rebellion (October-December 1857) was, in fact, a continuum of the risings of the period 1827-1857. The Rebellion of 1857 heralded a new phase only in the aftermath of the release of Surendra Sai from Hazaribag jail. The non-violent nature of the rebellion of the people like non-payment of revenue, non-attendance in offices and petions and delegations to the British authorities has been shed welcome light in the present report. The period saw the gradual entry of all the privileged classes – *Zamindars, Gauntias, Muafi* holders and people when their estates and traditional privileges, were withdrawn or taxed and, importantly, lands granted to the premier deity of the Tract Samaleswari were taxed. Those actions hurt the socio-religious sentiment of all classes of people. Above all of those was the popular demand of restoration of Sambalpur Raj with a Chauhan king. How the neglect of all those brought the people closer has been surveyed in this Report.

Instead of solving the problems, the British Government, which had become panic-stricken, started preparing for confrontation. The modi operandi or war strategies of the rebels – the guerrilla warfare, construction of fortresses on hil passes, sliding of stones from the hills during the movement of Government army, cutting off the lines of communication and Dak between Sambalpur on one side and Cuttack, Ranchi and Raipur-Nagpur; looting, arson and murdering of Government supporters on the one hand, and the Government action to counter them with military actions on the other, became the hallmarks of the period. Despite presence of sufficient army and operations, things did not improve. The Deputy Commissioner of Sambalpur became so desperate that he wrote to the authorities to relieve him of his present assignment. It has been graphically mentioned. The deaths of Dr. Moore on Government side and Chhabil Sai on the rebel side brought the early period to a close. In fact, the Government had become so much crestfallen that they declared the latter as 'a great victory'.

The Later Phase of Rebellion (1858-60) began with extensive military operations of the Government to meet the rapidly growing disturbances and state of the insurgency. To set an example to the rebels, Kolabira was attacked and its *Zamindar* was hanged in February 1858, Debrigarh and Pahadsirgida fortresses were attacked, stern measures were taken by Commissioner Cockburn of Cuttck to suppress the Rebellion. *Zamindaris* were confiscated, *Zamindar* Dial Sardar of Kharsal, Madhu *Guntia* of Jujomora who was involved in Dr. Morre's death and some others were hanged, a large number of people were imprisoned, feudatory chiefs of adjacent States were warned/fined against any help to rebels. Cap. Forster, who took charge of Deputy Commissioner of Sambalpur in March, 1858, unleashed a reign of terror.

Despite the measures, the rebellion became widespread and extended to peripheral regions of Khariar, Nawapara, Bindra-Nawagarh, Sarangarh on the border of Sambalpur and Raipur. The rebels killed the British supporters like Maharaja Sai of Deori, raided Khullari. Kings and *Zamindars* like those of Khariar, Bindra-Nawagarh, Tanwat came out in support of rebels. The States of Bamra, Patna, Raigarh and Sarangarh became victims of frequent rebel depredations. All those developments have been discussed at length.

The turning point came with failure of the policy and removal of Forster and, appointment of Maj. H.B. Impey as Deputy Commissioner, Sambalpur who began with policy of moderation and conciliation towards rebels. Through ups and downs, with a few successes and more failures in the beginning – he could ultimately obtain the surrender of all principal leaders, except one or two, before his death in December 1863. The courses of pursuance of the policy, reactions to those from different quarters and ultimate success have been highlighted.

The turn of the tide, which came with the appointment of A.B. Cumberlege as Deputy Commissioner, Sambalpur in January, 1864, reversed the liberal policy of his predecessor Impey although situations did not require so. Within a few days after taking over charge, he planned and succeeded in his avowed objective with help of higher authorities, as it were, by hook or crook, to arrest all those leaders who had surrendered and settled peacefully. They were transferred to Raipur and punished severely with transportation of life and forfeiture of properties. Thus, he put a seal on what had already been ended, through revengeful action and, earned the encomium as the suppresser of Rebellion when there was little trace of it.

Thus the investigation proved to be rewarding in so far as it brought to light some of the hitherto unknown facts, analyzed them from different angles – political, socio-economic and geographic and filled up a desideratum. The role of *Zamindairs* of Sambalpur, which was vital but has been sidelined from the mainstream study of 1857 Mutiny of Central- Eaastern India has been duly assessed and, another glorious chapter has been added to the annals of the Rebellion.

GLOSSARY

Amla : Officer of lower rank, Clerk.

Bagari : Forced labour.

Bandobast : Land Settlement.

Barkandazee	:	Foot-soldier.
Bendra	:	British man or soldier (derogatorily so called by local people).
Bhandi	:	Hair-cutter.
Bhogra	:	Land enjoyed for service to god or government.
Budmash	:	Wicked.
Bustee	:	Residential area of low class people.
Chaprasee	:	Peon.
Chauki	:	Station (postal, police, army).
Chaukidar	:	Village watchman.
Dak	:	Postal correspondence.
Dakhlee	:	Cultivable land not considered as mauza or revenue unit.
Deheri	:	Village priest.
Dhobi	:	Washer man.
Dungri	:	Small hill/hillock.
Elaka	:	Region.
Gaddi/Gadi	:	Throne.
Garh	:	Fort/Fortress.
Garhttea	:	Estate holder (equivalent to Zamindar).
Gauda	:	Milkman.
Gauntia	:	Village headman.
Ghasia	:	Sweeper.

Hartal	:	Strike, Cease work.
Istahara	:	Notification.
Jagir	:	Land-grant.
Jama	:	Annual land revenue.
Jamanbandi	:	Deposit (of Land Revenue).
Jhankar	:	Village priest.
Jummah	:	Deposit.
Khalsa	:	Village in royal demesne British territory.
Khukhol	:	Royal Daggar.
Kist	:	Instalment.
Koss	:	About three kilometers.
Kutchery	:	Court.
Malguzar	:	Revenue Collector of village land.
Malguzari	:	Land Revenue.
Mouza	:	Revenue area consisting of one or several villages.
Moolkee	:	Local.
Maufee (muafi)	:	Revenue free land grant.
Maufidari (muafidari)	:	Holder of revenue free land grant.
Muktiar	:	Junior Pleader.
Munsi	:	Clerk.
Nariha	:	Village water-bearer.
Nazrana	:	Present.

Negi	:	Village land revenue accountant.
Paik	:	Foot soldier.
Paltan	:	Irregular British soldier.
Panchayat	:	Arbitration court of a village.
Pandit	:	A learned man.
Pattah	:	Guaranteed deed.
Puggrie	:	Turban.
Purwanah	:	Notice, Warrant.
Raj	:	Crown.
Raja	:	King.
Rani	:	Queen.
Rasad	:	Provision of ration for the officer.
Rayat (Ryot)	:	A cultivator paying revenue directly to Government.
Saheb	:	Englishman.
Salam	:	Respect.
Sawar	:	Horse-soldier.
Sayees	:	Horse-soldier.
Sebundy	:	Foot soldier.
Sipahi	:	Sepoy or soldier.
Talpattri	:	Letter on palm leaf.
Taluk	:	An estate, area.
Talukadar	:	The Officer in-charge of a Taluk.

Thana	:	Police Station.
Thikadar	:	Contractor of land revenue, sometimes an intermediary between peasant and Zamindar.
Urzie	:	Representation/Petition.
Vakeel	:	Pleader.
Zamindar	:	Proprietor of an estate who pays revenue directly to the government.
Zamindari	:	The estate of a Zamindar.

BIBLIOGRAPHY

PRIMARY SOURCES

Official Sources

A. Records and Reports

Administration Department, *Bengal and Madras Papers.*

National Archives of India, New Delhi.

______. *Bengal and Miscellaneous Papers,* National Archives of India,

New Delhi.

______. *Feudatory Persons in British Jails,* National Archives of India,

New Delhi.

______. *General Administration,* Orissa State Archives, Bhubaneswar.

______. *Report on the territories of the Raja of Nagpur,* R. Jenkins,

Orissa State Archives, Bhubaneswar.

______. *Revenue regarding transfer of Sambalpur to Bengal,*

Orissa State Archives, Bhubaneswar.

______. *Sunnuds to Chiefs,* Orissa State Archives, Bhubaneswar.

______. *Supplement of the Report on the territories of the Raja of Nagpur,*

R. Jenkins, Nagpur Secretariat Record Room, Nagpur.

______. *Zamindaries and other petty Chieftainships,* R. Temple, Nagpur

Secretariat Record Room, Nagpur.

Foreign Department. *A note on Sambalpur Garjat Chiefs relating to the ancestors of the Chiefs of Sambalpur and that of Surendra Sai,* Orissa State Archives, Bhubaneswar.

______. *Arresting offenders in neighbouring native states,* National Archives of India, New Delhi.

______. *Bengal Papers relating to the Maratha War in 1803,* Printed by order of the House of Commons, West Bengal State Archives, West Bengal.

______. *Brindaban Das of Talsirgida,* Orissa State Archives, Bhubaneswar.

______. *General History of Sambalpur of the period beginning from 1818 to 1864,* Orissa State Archives, Bhubaneswar.

______. *Release of Dhanu Sai and Mitrabhanu Sai,* National Archives of India, New Delhi.

______. *Rewards to Narayan and Mohan Gountia of Lachhida,* National Archives of India, New Delhi.

______. *Surrender of Kanhai Naik of Kolabira and other rebels in 1861,* National Archives of India, New Delhi.

Home Department, *Bheden Zamindari,* Orissa State Archives, Bhubaneswar.

______. *Bizepur Zamindari,* Orissa State Archives, Bhubaneswar.

______. *Disagreement between Zamindars of Barpali, Patkulanda and Bizepur and other Gauntias,* Orissa State Archives, Bhubaneswar.

______. *Ghens Estate,* Orissa State Archives, Bhubaneswar.

_____. Indebtedness of Gauntias of Sambalpur,

Orissa State Archives, Bhubaneswar.

_____. *Kodabaga State,* Orissa State Archives, Bhubaneswar.

Home Judiciary Department, *Judicial Conspiracy of Surendra Sai,*

Orissa State Archives, Bhubaneswar.

_____. *Judgment of prisoners relating to Surendra Sai,*

Orissa State Archives, Bhubaneswar.

_____. *Garjat States of Patna,* Maj. H.B. Impey,

Orissa State Archives, Bhubaneswar.

_____. *General History of Sambalpur of the period beginning from 1818 to*

1864 Orissa State Archives, Bhubaneswar.

_____. *Survey of Nagpur States down to 1854,* Capt. G. Ramsay,

Madhya Pradesh State Archives, Bhopal.

_____. *Studies on the Restoration of the State,*

Orissa State Archives, Bhubaneswar.

B. Gazetteers

De Brett, E.A. *Chhatisgarh Feudatory States Gaztteer* (1878).

Grant, C. *The Gazetteer of the Central Provinces of India* (1870).

O' Malley, L.S.S. *Bihar Orissa District Gazetteer-Sambalpur* (1932).

_____. *Bengal District Gazetteer – Sambalpur (1909).*

Behuria, H.C.(ed). *Orissa State Gazetteers,* 3 Vols (Bhubaneswar 1991-92).

Ramsey, L.E.B. *Bengal Gazetteers.*

_____. *Feudatory States of Orissa* (1870).

Senapati, N.(ed). *Orissa District Gazetteers – Sambalpur* (1971), Balangir (1968), Kalahandi (1980).

C. Letters

Board of Revenue Record, Sambalpur –

Letter No. Nil, dated 26.1.2.1818; Letter No. Nil, dated 16.6.1832;

Letter No. Nil, dated 23.7.1832; Letter No. 4457, dated 15.12.1851;

Letter No. 171, dated 5.5.1854; Letter No. 41, dated 15.8.1857;

Letter No. 43, dated 22.8.1857; Letter No. Nil, dated 7.9.1857;

Letter No. 45, dated 10.9.1857; Letter No. Nil, dated 6.10.1857;

Letter No. Nil, dated 8.10.1857; Letter No. Nil, dated 17.10.1857;

Letter No. Nil, dated 30.10.1857; Letter No. Nil, dated 1.11.1857;

Letter No. 211, dated 4.11.1857; Letter No. 98, dated 4.11.1857;

Letter No. Nil, dated 7.11.1857; Letter No. Nil, dated 26.11.1857;

Letter No. 306, dated 3.12.1857; Letter No. Nil, dated 5.12.1857;

Letter No. Nil, dated 7.12.1857; Letter No. 4457, dated 13.12.1857;

Letter No. 94, dated 30.12.1857; Letter No. Nil, dated 3.12.1864.

Madhya Pradesh State Archives, Bhopal –

Letter No. 76, dated 28.7.1860; Letter No. 495, dated 28.7.1860;

Letter No. 6, dated 8.8.1860; Letter No. Nil, dated 26.8.1860;

Letter No. Nil, dated 8.9.1860; Letter No. 10, dated 12.11.1860;

Letter No. Nil, dated 28.8.1862; Letter No. 38, dated 19.1.1864;

Letter No. 38, dated 23.1.1864; Letter No.110, dated 25.1.1864;

Letter No. Nil, dated 1.2.1864; Letter No. Nil, dated 3.2.1864;

Letter No. Nil, dated 11.2.1864; Letter No. Nil, dated 22.12.1864;

Letter No. 1864, dated 20.1.1865.

National Archives of India, New Delhi –

Letter No. Nil, dated 27.2.1833; Letter No. Nil, dated 30.5.1833;

Letter No. Nil, dated 21.6.1833; Letter No. Nil, dated 22.6.1833;

Letter No. Nil, dated 27.6.1833; Letter No. Nil, dated 2.8.1833;

Letter No. Nil, dated 13.9.1833; Letter No. Nil, dated 13.10.1833;

Letter No. Nil, dated 13.10.1833; Letter No. 103, dated 6.2.1834;

Letter No. 1, dated 12.12.1849; Letter No. 1, dated 3.1.1850;

Letter No. 3, dated 9.1.1850; Letter No. 10, dated 3.2.1850;

Letter No. 33, dated 6.3.1850; Letter No. 19, dated 6.3.1850;

Letter No. 8, dated 6.10.1850; Letter No. 4, dated 12.1.1851;

Letter No. Nil, dated 19.3.1851; Letter No. 109, dated 10.3.1852;

Letter No. 33, dated 22.5.1852; Letter No. 2185, dated 24.8.1860;

Letter No. C, dated 16.5.1862; Letter No. 60, dated 25.5.1862;

Letter No. 657, dated 15.7.1862; Letter No. 4035, dated 12.9.1863;

Letter No. 1, dated 12.11.1863; Letter No. C, dated 22.1.1864;

Letter No. 3523, dated 1.8.1864; Letter No. Nil, dated 2.12.1864;

Letter No. 462, dated 22.2.1866.

Nagpur Secretariat Record Room, Nagpur –

Letter No. Nil, dated 23.7.1862; Letter No. 908, dated - 1865.

Orissa State Archives, Bhubaneswar –

Letter No. Nil, dated 30.7.1842; Letter No. Nil, dated 13.8.1842;

Letter No. 3119, dated 15.10.1857; Letter No. 87, dated 23.10.1857;

Letter No. 214, dated 6.11.1857; Letter No. Nil, dated 16.12.1857;

Letter No. Nil, dated 27.12.1857; Letter No. 1, dated 15.2.1858;

Letter No. Nil, dated 3.3.1858; Letter No. Nil, dated 13.6..1858;

Letter No. 237, dated 14.10.1858; Letter No. 77, dated 28.7.1860;

Letter No. 5580, dated 19.11.1860; Letter No. Nil, dated 20.1.1861;

Letter No. Nil, dated 8.6.1861; Letter No. Nil, dated 7.8.1861;

Letter No. Nil, dated 11.12.1861; Letter No. Nil, dated 17.12.1861;

Letter No. 4353, dated 26.12.1861; Letter No. Nil, dated 28.12.1861;

Letter No. Nil, dated 21.1.1862; Letter No. 8, dated 27.1.1862;

Letter No. Nil, dated 2.2.1862; Letter No. Nil, dated 14.2.1862;

Letter No. 18, dated 24.2.1862; Letter No. Nil, dated 25.2.1862;

Letter No. Nil, dated 31.3.1862; Letter No. Nil, dated 14.4.1862;

Letter No. 109, dated 21.5.1862; Letter No. Nil, dated 30.8.1862;

Letter No. Nil, dated 12.12.1863; Letter No. 186, dated 24.1.1864;

Letter No. 110, dated 25.1.1864.

West Bengal State Archives, West Bengal –

Letter No. 1474, dated 18.3.1833.

SECONDARY SOURCES

Books

Aitchison, C.U. *A Collection of Treaties, Engagements and Sanads Relating to India and Neighbouring Countries.* Vol. II, Calcutta, 1930

Banerjee, S.N. *A Nation in the Making* (New Delhi, 1963).

Bose, S.C. *The Indian Struggle* (Bombay, 1947).

Buckland, C.E. *Bengal under the Lieutenant Governors* (Calcutta, 1901).

Chopra, P.N. (ed). *Who's Who of Indian Martyrs,* Vol. IIII (New Delhi, 1973).

Das, A. *Life of Surndra Sai* (Cuttack, 1963).

Das, S. *Chauhan Veera Surendra Sai* (Cutack, 1958).

Das, S.P. *Sambalpurar Itihas* (Sambalpur, 1962).

Dash, Pt. S.N. *Odishare Sipahi Vidrohara Jhalaka* (Cuttack, 1955).

Dey, S.C. *Guide to Orissa Records*, 5 Vols. (Bhubaneswar, 1967).

______. *Who's Who of Freedom Movement in Orissa,* 5 Vols. (Bhubaneswar, 1969)

Fraser, H.L. *Among ndian Rajahs and Ryots* (London, 1912).

Guru, G.P. (ed). *West Orissa : Past and Present,* (Bhubaneswar, 2009).

Hasan, K. *Sambal;purara Swadhinata Sangramo* (Sambalpur University, 2001).

Hunter, W.W. *History of Orissa,* 2 Vols. (London, 1872).

King, A.F. *Early Records of British India* (Calcutta, 1876).

Lakshminarasiah, P. *Encyclopedia of Bengal, Bihar and Orissa* (Madras,

    1924-25).

Mahatab, H.K. *History of Orissa,* 2 Vols. (Cuttack, 1959).

Majumdar, B.C. *Sone;pur in Sambal;pur Tract* (Clcutta, 1911).

Mishra, C.R. *Freedom Movement in Sambalpur 1827-1942.*

Mishra, D.B. *Concise History of Orissa* (New Delhi, 2005).

Mishra, J. "Sangrami Balabhadra Singh Deo", *Gana Istahar,* pp.3-4,

    14 Nov. 2008

Mishra, R.K. *Surendra Sai Pioneer of a Complete Revolution (1857),*

    Sambalpur, 2002.

Mukherjee, P. *History of Orissa in the 19th Century,* (Cuttack, 1964),

    Utkal University History of Orissa, Vol. VI, (Bhubaneswar, 1964).

Patra, K.M. *Orissa Under the East India Company* (New Delhi, 1971).

Sahu, N.K. *Veer Surendra Sai* (Bhubaneswar, 1985).

Sahu, J.K. *Veer Surendra Sai* (Cuttack, 1998).

Sinha, H.N. *Report on the Sambalpur Garjat States* (Bengal Selection No.III, 1851).

Supkar, K. (ed). *Sambalpurara Parichaya* (Sambalpur, 2008).

Willis, C.U. *British Relation with Nagpur Status* (Year and date not known).

Unpublished Dissertation

Sahu,J.K. "Chauhan Rule in Western Orissa" (Ph.D.thesis, Utkal University,

    1964)

Articles

Das, S. "Surndra Sainika atmasarmarpana", *Navajivan,* Vol.II, 1957, pp.594-596.

______. "Surendra Sainika Vyaktivtva", *Navajivian,* Vol. II, 1957, pp. 502-504.

Das, S.P. "The Patna State and the Sambalpur Raj", *Journal of Kalinga Historical Research Society,* (Bolangir), Vol. II, 1950, pp. 235-242.

______. "Unknown King of Sambalpur", *Proceedings of Orissa Historical Congress* (Puri), Vol. II, 1970, pp. 17-20.

Mishra, C.R. "Spirit of Freedom : An Overview of popular Movements in the Sambalpur Region", *West Orissa : A Study in Ethos,* Sambalpur University, 1992.

Mohanty, R.R. "Bharatara Mukti Sangrama pain ladhithiba Paschima Odishara Pramukha sangramee gana", *The Samaj,* 26 Jan. 2001.

Mukharjee, P. "Surendra Sai", *Navajivan,* Vol I, 1957, pp. 865-872.

Panda, S.C. "Veer Surendra Sai", *New Aspects of History of Orissa*, p. 23, Sambalpur University, 1985.

Sahu, J.K. "Paschima Odishara Swadhinata Sangrama O Saheed Kamal Singh Dao", *Chetana Vartta*, Vol. 2, No. 2, June 2003.

Sahu, N.K. "Ratna Kumasi", *Saptarshi* (Sambalpur), Vol. II, 1972, pp. 14-27.

______. "Sambalpur through Ages", *Orissa Historical Congress* (Sambalpur), Vol. II, 1970, pp. 1-10.

Magazines/Journals/Periodicals

Agnisikha (weekly), Sambalpur, 1962-1967.

Asha (weekly), Berhampur, 1913-1936.

Jagarana (weekly), Sambalpur, 1936-1938.

Journal of Asiatic Society Bengal (Calcutta).

Navajivan (monthly), Cuttack.

Proceedings Orissa History Congress.

Prajatantra (weekly), Balasore, 1916-1935.

Sadhana (weekly), Sambalpur, 1922-1927.

Samaj (weekly-daily), Puri, Cuttack, 1919-1947.

Sambadabahika (weekly), Balasore, 1872-1923.

Sambalpur Hitaisini (weekly), Bamrah State, 1895-1922.

Saptarshi, Sambalpur University Journal, August 1972,

   May and November 1974; March and June 1977, January, May,

   October, December 1978.

Seva (weekly), Sambalpur, 1921-1922.

Utkala Darpana, Sambalpur.

Utkala Dipika (weekly), Cuttack, 1869-1833.

Utkala Sahitya (monthly), Cuttack.

Utkala Sevaka (weekly), Sambalpur.

Souvenir, *Veer Surendra Sai Bicentenary Birth Anniversary Celebration*

(ed. Dani, P.S., Odisha Sanskrutika Samaj, Sambalpur, 2009).

Souvenir, *Veer Surendra Sai Bicentenary Birth Anniversary Celebration*

Committee, (ed. Dhar, S.S., Sambalpur, 2009).

Utkal Prasanga, Surendra Sai Special, April, 1984.

The Feudatory and Zamindari India (Trichinapaly November, 1935).

Odisha Review

Jatiya Veer Surendra Sai, Sambalpur, 1984.

Miscellaneous

Azadi Express : 2007. Photo Exhibition of the Freedom Struggle.

Two *Pamphlets* : Upapdhyay, M. The 1857 Great March Meerut to

Delhi

&

Azadi Express : Eka Drishtipat (Oriya)
By
Ministry of Information and Broadcasting, Government of India,
New Delhi, 2007.

APPENDIX-I

Glimpses of the 1857 Mutiny in the Folk songs of

Sambalpur Tract

The spirit of resistance and fighting against the British Government as well as references to some important incidents and personages have been found in the folk songs which are quite large in the Sambalpur Tract. In the process of running down from generation to generation over the century and a half many of them have been lost to posterity because they remained oral traditions in local dialect (*Sambalpuri*) which has been in a unwritten state till very late. Besides no systematic attempt has been made to collect them from various parts of the tract and compile them so that these can be used as a strand of the sources. However those, which are available, have been perused in the present investigation, which sometimes are of inestimable help as those shed welcome light on some obscure facts and sometimes replenish or corroborate facts gleaned from other dependable written documents. A few illustrations of them, with English translation, are given in the following pages.

A good number of folk songs about Ghens *Zamindar* family are current. The bravery of Kunjel Singh while guarding the Singhora pass on Sambalpur- Nagpur road is sung as follows:

Aam Khaeli Jam Khaeli Pakei Deli Tanko,

Bandh Talar Kagaj Patar Sundar Barihake Dako,

Sundar Bariha Baela Bhai Patna Kete Dhur,

Apen Raja Bije Kale Baud Nagar.

Baud Nagpurun Patna Sdak Dan Tala,

Bhitre Bhitre Kunjal Singh Raeje Matala.

Kei Dela Gur-Ganjei, Ki Dela Chura,

Singhda Ghatine Margala Jaiphula Kara Paen,

Mukut Bandha Ghuda Ho ...

[I took mangoes, black-berrys and threw away seeds. You call Sunder Beriha to come with records of the land below the tank. Sunder Beriha told, Oh brothers! Our king has gone to (as far as) Baudh and Nagpur. Kunjel Singh has secretly fomented (rebellion) in the state, the whole route Baud-Nagpur-Patna started shaking in commotion. Some gave *gur* (molasses), some *ganjei* (hemp) some gave *chura* (a paddy preparation called 'poha' in Hindi). At Singohra pass was killed the crowned horse(the British soldiers).

On 27.1.2.1857, there was a serve fight between Madho Singh and British troops led by Capt. E.G. Wood at Singhora pass. Many English soldiers were killed. But Capt. Wood escaped to Sambalpur and saved his life. After nearly one year, Madho Singh was caught in the month of December, 1858 and hanged to death. At the aged of 72 he became a martyr. His memory is still cherished in the heart of the people in the form of folksongs:

Tal-Bandh Upar-Bandh Kalgarngar Bhadi,

Bhojpurar Abujh Kandh, Pakdei Dela Khadi,

Kaen Karba Duan Babu Dihen Naina Adi,

Taha Suni Duan Babu Hela Jajrman,

Asin Mase Kagaj Pesla Madho Bariha Than.

Madho Bariha Baela Bhai Tame Kanthi, Dia Kanthi,

Sabu Lskar Palei Gale Singhdamuhanr Ghati,

Dia Guli Chalei Gusein Dia Guli Chalei.

[The Diwan became enraged to hear the disturbance of Abujh Kond. He sent papers to Madho Singh in the month of Aswin. Madho said, brother, you raise wall. All the soldiers have gone to Singhora pass. Start firing at them].

There was a dispute between Ghess *Zamindar* Madho Singh and Bijepur *Zamindar* over Bhatibahal region. Bijepur *Zamindar* was acting as an informer of the British Government. He informed the Britishers about the rebellious activities of Madho Singh and his family. Earlier, Madho Singh opposed the policy of the British Government and also did not pay the enhanced revenue. On the other hand, he joined hands with Surendra Sai and fought against the Britishers.

When a list of defaulters was prepared by the Britishers in order to confiscate their property, Madho Singh's name was found at the top of the roll. Bijepur *Zamindar* was very clever and smart. He took advantage of that situation and rushed to Sambalpur to justify his claim over Bhatibahal region. The British supported his claim to award Bhatibahal to Bijepur *Zamindar* and amalgamated that area with his estate. This incident has been mockingly depicted in the following folksong:

Gand Madhyen Binjhar Bhadi Kabri Naik Thai,

Bijepuria Arjit Kala Samalpure Jai,

Nei Ja Tor Puo Prja, Nei Ja Tor Bhuin,

Ghess Jamidar Mare Muin Nain Parli Rahi,

Ghui Bagir Nuruachhe Mate Juhi Juhi,

Jiban Thile Jibka Achhe, Jauiphula Karapean,

Magi Khaemi Muin Ho ...

Participation

The resistance against the British took a violent turn in Sambalpur when Surendra Sai and some of his rebel colleagues took part and headed the movement. All those who have gone to fight against the Britishers have been given the status of brothers by the village girls in the folk songs. The following example of *Humo Bauli* song reveals this:

Semi Phul Kera Kera Baulare,

Semi Phul Kera Kera,

Mor Dada Jauchhe Sipei Dera,

Lokmane Tara Tara Baulire

Lokmane Tara Tara re …

[Oh playmate (friend), the bean flowers have grown in bunches. My brother has gone to the camp of the sepoys (fight against them). The people are astonished (afraid of) (to know) of it].

Kodopali Battle

The most ghastly battle took place in Kudopali on 10.12.1857. It is a memorable episode not only in the history of Sambalpur but in the history of Freedom Movement in India. Captain E.G. Wood besieged the rebel stronghold of Kudopli. The rebels met with their first major debacle at this point. As many as 53 revolutionaries were killed in this battle. Subsequently, six captured from Kudopali battle were hanged. It is true that nowhere in Orissa so many revolutionaries were killed in a single action during that period. Chhabila Sai was the fifth brother of Surendra Sai. He was shot in the back while he was running away to catch his horse. The event became an immortal part of folklore for ever.

Uli Uli Uli Uli Baulire,

Uli Uli Uli Uli

Chhabila Sai Dihen Bajila Guli,

Chhabila Sai Dihen Bajila Guli,

Kudopali Majha Khuli Baulire,

Kudopali Majha Khuli re...

[*Uli, Uli* is a form of exclamation. The bullet (of the British) has shot Chhabila on the main lane of Kudopali].

During this historical period of fighting against the Britishers, some were also acting as informers of Britishers. For example, Dayanidhi Meher, who gave information against Surendra Sai. This incident has been depicted sarcastically in the following Jaiphula folk song:

Jaiphula Lo, jai Janglia Kanta,

Saheba Deichhe Muthae Tanka Muthae Tanka,

Jaiphula Lo, Khagla Phitai Paka,

Benkar Khagla Jhaakamaka,

Jaiphula Lo, Rani Bandh Jhakamaka.

[Oh friend! The Saheb (British official) has given a handful of rupees (to the informer). Throw away your neck-wears(as in shame)].

Madho Singh, a supporter of the legitimate claim of Surendra Sai to the throne of Sambalpur was sure that the latter who was interned at Hazaribag jail for his revolution by the British Government at the instance of Narayan Singh – the king of Sambalpur – would return one day and resume his fighting. [Madho learnt the release of Surendra from the jail. He ordered the blacksmith Madhu to prepare weapons and forge iron balls of the size of palm, out of worn-out spades sickles, axes and plough-shares, for the ensuing fighting which has been described below].

I Kathata Ghens Zamindar

Sor paigale

Macdhu luhurake daki kari

Ades deidele |

Jahathile thute kued

Thunthi kasana luha anidiele

Chapar ede ede gula tiyar kar baile |

Suni kari Madhu luhura

Sajbaj hela

Thunthi da tangarke

Bhala tiar kala.

[The brave fighting of the two brothers Hatte and Kunjel in which they shot at the eyes of the British soldiers who fell down at Singhora pass and, as it were, they were given as sacrifices to the numen, *Ghens Mata* as sung below].

Hatte Singh ar Kunjel Singh

Duhen bandhle juli

Gora Sarkarke marinele

Ainkh chahata juli

Guli gala chali

Saheb gala dhali

Ghens Matana nei kari

Dei dele bali ||

[Hatte Singh invoked deities of the *Zamindari* like *Ghens Mata, Budharaja, Guhal Gusian, Andheripat, Chhatarbairag, Patmesari* etc. to protect him in his fighting against the British who he wanted to kill has been found in the following folk song. Hatte Singh thereafter fired the cannons which fell on the *Paltans* (irregular soldiers) like showers of the month of Shravan].

Juhar karuchhen Ghens Matago

Juhar karuchhen tate

Gura sarkarke marmi

Shaha heithibu mate |

Juhar karuchhen Budharaja

Tui ta gaonr raja

Ghudar upare chadhi bullu

Dekshale puo parja

Tor daya hale Mago

Gura Sarkarke marmi

Tor gachhe loti kari

Mud ulei demi

Juhar karucche Rait-Mait

Tor daya thile

Dinarbele rait hesi

Tui daya kale

Juhar Mago Guha Gosian

Tui ta Dasmati

Tor daya hele Mago

Nai pade bipatti

Juhar Mago Andharipat

Daya rakhithibu mate

Bipae padlen saha hebu

Juhar karuchhen tate

Juhar karuchhen Chhatar Bairag

Bat batanu tui

Jen bate shatru ailen deuthiibu kahi

Juhar Juhar Patmesiri go

Tui ta savur mul

Kete dev devta tor thane

Heichhan go thul

Tor daya hale Mago

Raij muin jitami

Sul dinke sul puja

Bali deuthime

Ete bali Hathe Singh

Top dele jali

Sravan masar varsa bagir

Gule gala padi

Jaha thile paltan mane

Padle muha madi

[The following song describes the fighting of Hathe Singh and Kunjal in a marvelous way. It probably relates to the time following the hanging of Madho Singh in 1858. The valiant Hatte Singh became enraged and ordered Pharikar, Laksman Karare, Manglu Jhankar to come forward with their arms and weapons to finish off the Bendras (British). Some came out with swords some with battle-axe, some with javelins. Some filled the cannons with balls. They waited for the arrival of the Bendras (British forces) to come to the Andhrei Burei (groove) of Ghens. When the latter came, the former fired from the ambush. Some men of the forces were slain, some were injured and some retreated. Kunjal Singh chased and killed a few from Lakhapakhnu to Bhaten Dungri].

Rage tharhar hei kari Hatte Singh veer

Bendra ke marbar lagi dakle Phrikar

Lakshman Karari Manglu Thenkar adi kete veer

Hatte Singh kahuchhan sun Pharikar

Hat hatiar jaha achhe bahar kar

Kie dhaila khanda tangi kie dhaile varchhi

Kada bind topthe kie gula kala bharthi

Tahum bahar hoile Ghens Zamindar

Andhrei burei the jai lukle dhari Pharikar

x   x   x   x   x

x   x   x   x   x

Ghuda pinda chadhi kari paltan aile dhain

Ghens Zamindar lukichhe bali takar jana nai ||

Paltan shabad paikari

Hatte Singh veer

Tupe gula bhari kari

Chhadi dele thir

Sailta dela jali

Dho dho tho tho top gal phuthi ||

The sacrifices and suffering of the members of Ghens *Zamindar* family have been immortalized, in the following songs which sings the death of Airi Singh, the transportation of Hate Singh (to Kalapani or Andamans), the execution of Kunjal and the death of Bairi Singh of small-pox in Sambalpur jail.

Sai juli luki thila

Airi Singh mala

Nai hagtla Hatte Singh

Dipantar ke gala

Kalia ghudar jan

Madho Singhar panchata khute

Dhan mor banchla Nagen

Mechha anthi jivan dela mudkata

Ghensar Juan (Kunjal)

Hatte Singh ke Kalapain

Kunjal Singh ke phasi

Baira Singh Sambalpur

Matathi pahadi gala

[Courtesy: The first six songs from *West Orissa : Past and Present(ed. G.P.Guru)* and the rest from *Souvenir, Veer Suirendra Sai Birth Bi-Centenary*

APPENDIX – II

FACSIMILES OF SOME IMPORTANT LETTERS

1. D.O. letter of Captain Leigh to Captin Dalton

2. D.O. letter dt. 28 Aug. 1857 of Captain Leigh

3. Letter of Capt. Leigh to the Commissioner of Nagpur

4. Sketch map of the place where Capt. Woodbridge was killed as prepared by J.P. Ensign Warlow, Offier Commanding.

5. D.O. letter of Captain Leigh to Captin Dlton.

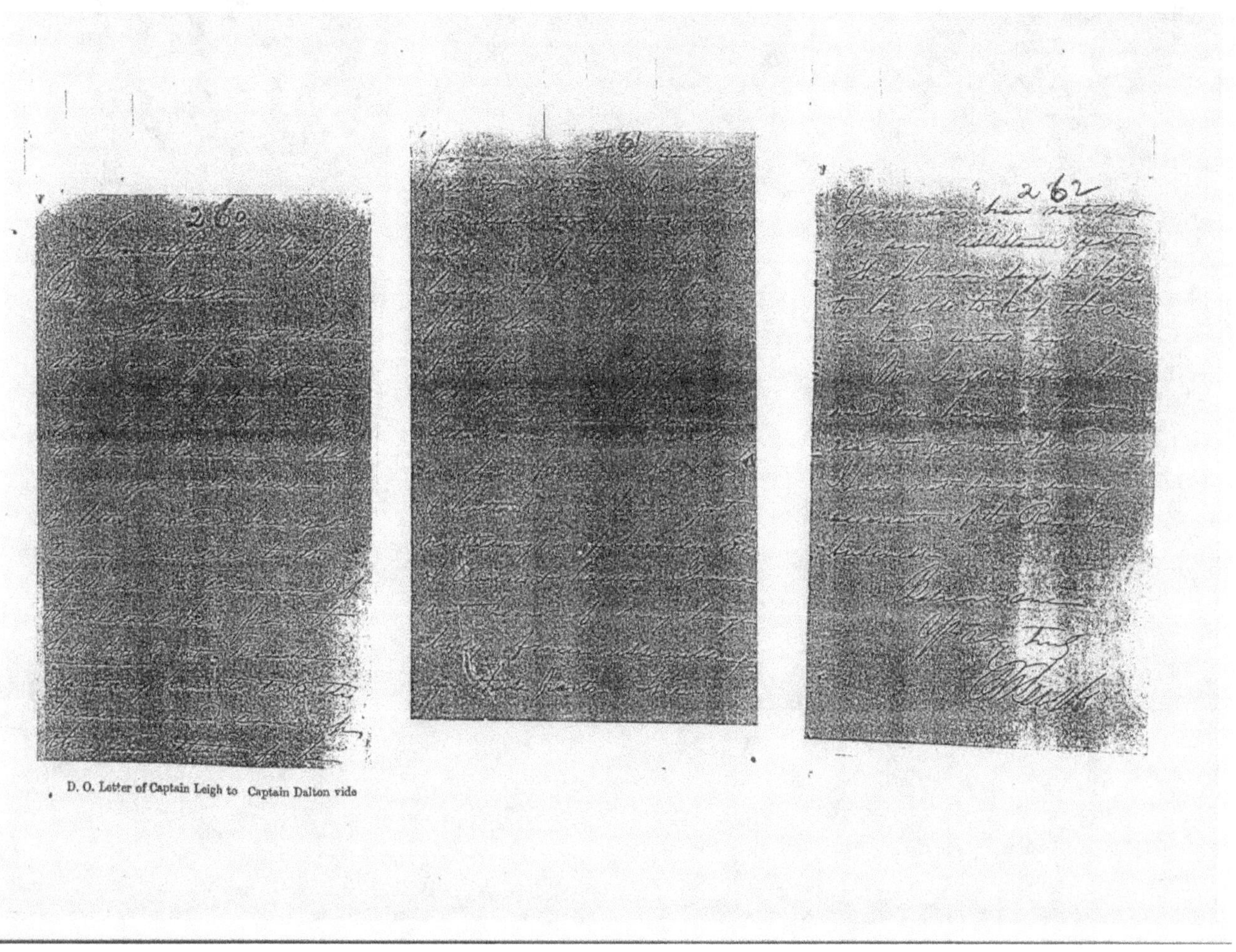

D. O. Letter of Captain Leigh to Captain Dalton vide

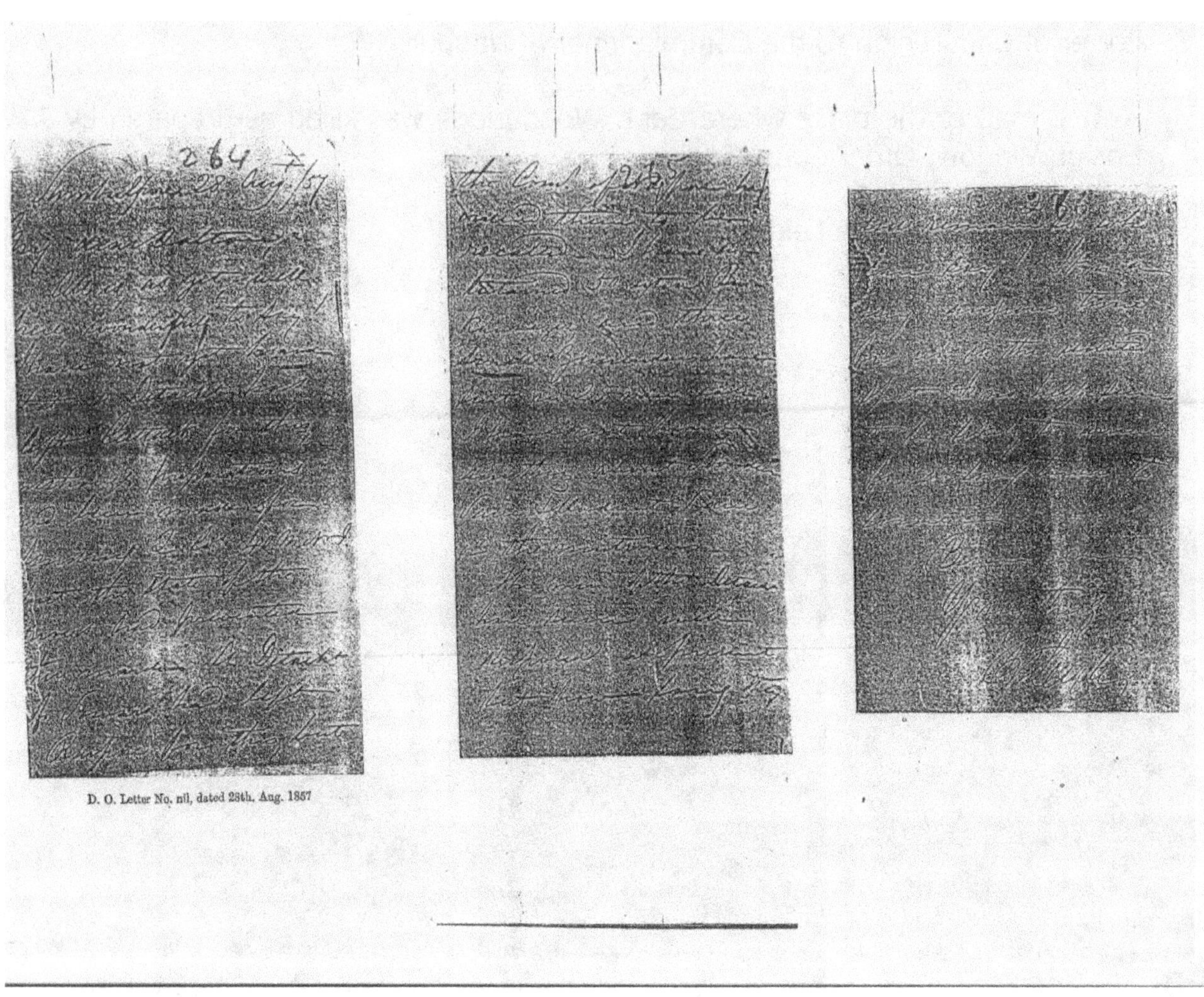

D. O. Letter No. nil, dated 28th. Aug. 1857

Letter of Capt. L igh to the commissioner Nagpur.

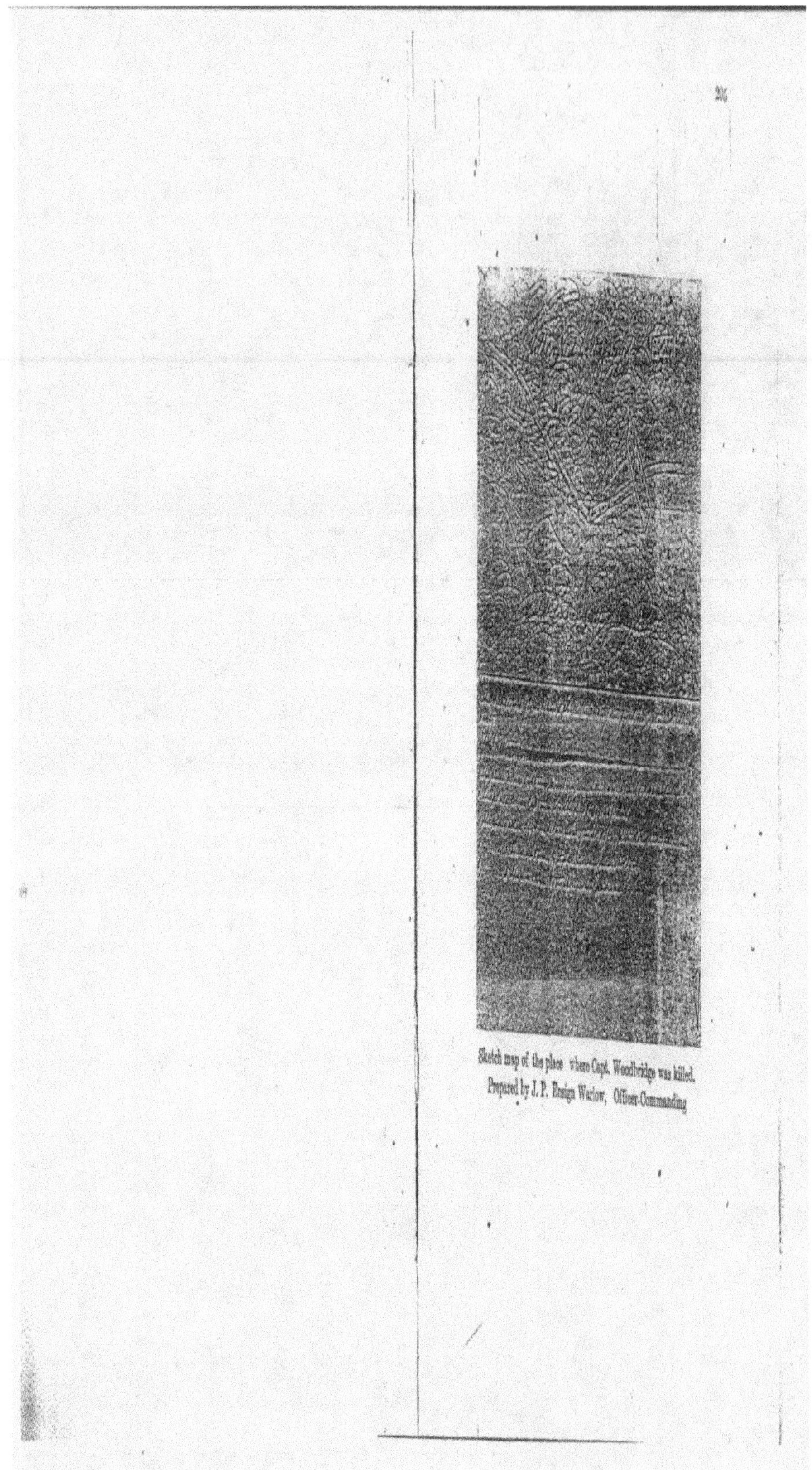

Sketch map of the place where Capt. Woodbridge was killed.
Prepared by J. P. Ensign Warlow, Officer-Commanding

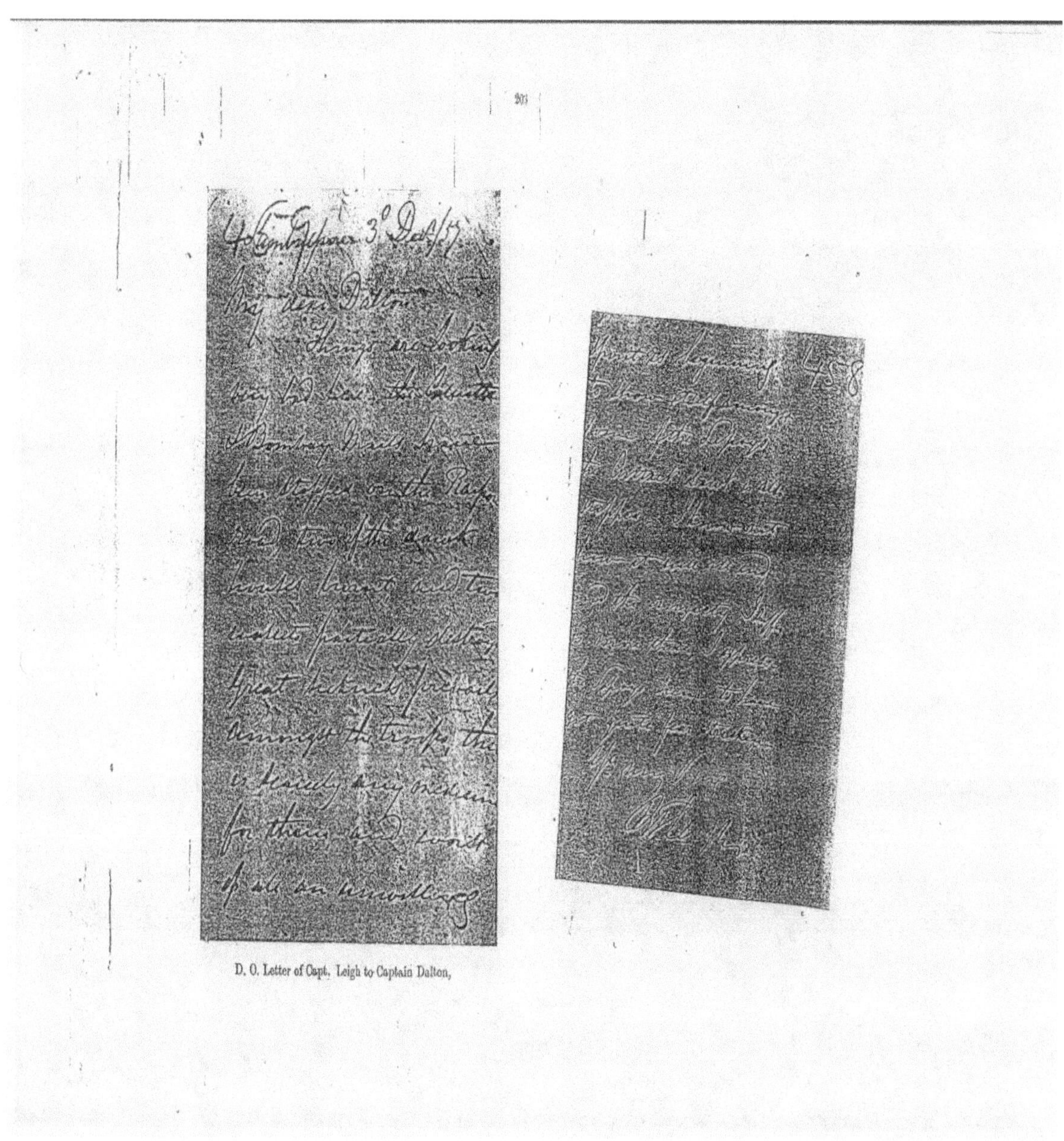

D. O. Letter of Capt. Leigh to Captain Dalton,